THE
WORD'S
OUT

Praise for *The Word's Out*

'David and Paul brilliantly chart how Christian movements and practices, current cultural context and biblical interpretation have shaped and continue to shape our understanding of evangelism. This great book helps us to decipher a clearer view of effective evangelism today, which at its simplest is to learn from Jesus' example.'

Rachel Jordan, National Mission and Evangelism Advisor to the Church of England

'When I read *The Word's Out*, three things resonated immediately: that it is realistic, holistic and focused on a local-church approach to evangelism. These are three significant factors in our evangelism at Christians in Sport and this book has become a core work in our training curriculum.'

Graham Daniels, General Director, Christians in Sport

'This is that rare thing – a book on evangelism that is theologically rich, culturally aware and earthily practical at the same time. It deserves careful reading and is an important contribution to our understanding of this vital ministry in the church.'

Graham Tomlin, Bishop of Kensington

'We need all the help we can get to enable ordinary people from all sorts of churches to enjoy sharing their faith: bring it on!'

Lucy Moore, Messy Church Team Leader at BRF

The Bible Reading Fellowship
15 The Chambers, Vineyard
Abingdon OX14 3FE
brf.org.uk

The Bible Reading Fellowship (BRF) is a Registered Charity (233280)

ISBN 978 0 85746 816 1
Second edition published 2019
First edition published 2013
10 9 8 7 6 5 4 3 2 1 0
All rights reserved

Text © David Male and Paul Weston 2013, 2019
This edition © The Bible Reading Fellowship 2019
Cover illustration by Rebecca J Hall

Acknowledgements
Unless otherwise stated, scripture quotations are taken from the New Revised Standard Version
of the Bible, Anglicised Edition, copyright © 1989, 1995 by the Division of Christian Education of
the National Council of the Churches of Christ in the United States of America, and are used by
permission. All rights reserved.

Scripture quotations marked NIV are taken from The Holy Bible, New International Version
(Anglicised edition). Copyright © 1979, 1984, 2011 by Biblica (formerly International Bible Society).
Used by permission of Hodder & Stoughton Publishers, an Hachette UK company. All rights
reserved. 'NIV' is a registered trademark of Biblica (formerly International Bible Society). UK
trademark number 1448790.

Scripture quotations marked RSV are taken from The Revised Standard Version of the Bible,
copyright © 1946, 1952, 1971 by the Division of Christian Education of the National Council of the
Churches of Christ in the United States of America, are used by permission. All rights reserved.

A catalogue record for this book is available from the British Library

Printed and bound in Great Britain by Clays Ltd, Elcograf S.p.A.

THE
WORD'S
OUT

Principles and strategies for effective evangelism today

Revised and updated edition

David Male and Paul Weston

Foreword by
Justin Welby, Archbishop of Canterbury

Acknowledgements

This book came out of a friendship that has developed over the past 30 years, nine of which were shared as colleagues at Ridley Hall, Cambridge. We thank our colleagues and former students there, as well as at Church House, who have encouraged and influenced us. Among the many writers and speakers who have impacted us, we particularly thank the evangelists and church leaders who have personally inspired us in our ministries, especially John Finney, Michael Green, Vic Jackopson, Lesslie Newbigin, Gavin Reid, Roger Simpson and David Watson.

Thank you, too, to the participants on the CPAS Arrow Leadership Programme, where David road-tested some of his material, and to friends and supporters of the Newbigin Centre in Cambridge who have been a constant encouragement to Paul. Thank you to those who, in many different ways, got the word out to us that we might hear about Jesus and respond to him. Thank you to the people at BRF. A particular thank you to Justin Welby for writing the Foreword to this second edition.

Finally, thanks to our families, who have supported and encouraged us, especially of course our wives, Heather and Ginny.

David Male and Paul Weston

Contents

Foreword to the new edition

What I like about this book is that it's not about the authors.

Don't get me wrong; I was delighted when Dave Male became head of the Discipleship and Evangelism Department for the Church of England, and I have known of Paul Weston's teaching for some time. But what I mean is that this book is clearly written to make an impact – and that impact is not to be impressed at the achievements of the writers, but to be equipped to participate.

In writing this book, Dave and Paul have performed a service to the church – they have laid out the history and practice, the how, the what and the where of evangelism. And they have done it in an informative and stimulating way. But the main thing they have done is given fuel to the why of evangelism. The why is of course a who: Jesus Christ.

This book, then, is an answer to prayer, because we regularly pray that God would equip his church with tools for the joyful task of proclaiming Jesus. This book is ultimately about Jesus. I pray the fruit of it will be seen in lives and communities that are transformed by his love.

Justin Welby, Archbishop of Canterbury

Introduction

This book comes out of our longing to see the ministry of evangelism reinstated, re-energised and reinvigorated in the church today. It started life during conversations over staff coffee at Ridley Hall, with the observation that evangelism seemed to have a low level of credibility among many church leaders and members. Research done by the London Institute for Contemporary Christianity (LICC) in 2010, as part of its 'Imagine' Project, suggests that 'evangelism is seen by many as simply doing strange things to strange people in strange places' and finds that 'many Christians are uncomfortable with the idea of their life as a witness or reject the idea outright'. At a recent evangelism training event, a courageous person spoke for many present when he said, 'I know I should do evangelism, but I don't want to, and I feel guilty.'

Our great concern is that *this* is the moment at which the church most needs to be involved in effective evangelism. All the figures clearly indicate that most people in westernised nations have very little knowledge of the Christian story, and churchgoing is no longer part of mainstream culture for the great majority. Peter Brierley's work on church attendance in Britain over the last 30 years estimates that attendance as a percentage of the UK population has halved to 4.7%. Moreover, this churchgoing population is also an ageing population. According to the 2016 Mission Statistics of the Church of England, of those attending Anglican churches regularly, 20% were under the age of 18 and 31% were aged 70 or over.

Ironically, today we seem to have lots of talk about the importance of mission and yet very little about the priority of evangelism in our mission strategies. It can even seem at times as if the word 'missional' can encompass everything except evangelism. The

American market-research guru George Barna sums up the problem when he states, 'How ironic that during this period of swelling need for the proclamation of the gospel… the ranks of the messengers have dissipated to anaemic proportions.'[1]

Our simple conviction is that at a time when the church is declining quickly and also rapidly losing confidence in evangelism, the need to get 'the word out' is more pressing than ever. So how can we enable others to connect with Jesus and his people in meaningful ways? How can we introduce the good news in ways that engage rather than turn off our hearers? How can we think more constructively about how to engage our culture with the message of the gospel? What is certain is that we cannot afford simply to sit back and do nothing. This is a crucial time for the church to get the word out.

Our hope for this book, therefore, is that it will not only remind the church of the vital importance of evangelism but it will also suggest some ways forward in our thinking and practice. We long to see the church, across denominations and traditions, engaged in more effective evangelism and, through God's grace, seeing transformation in the lives of individuals and communities.

We have each contributed different parts of the book, although we freely commented on each other's work. We have found ourselves in broad agreement, even though, on detail, we may have differed.

After two introductory chapters (one by David on how we have arrived at our current position and the other by Paul on our culture's impact on the ways we engage in evangelism), the main body of the book is divided into two parts.

Paul has written Part 1, 'Evangelism and the New Testament'. His aim here has been to reflect on a number of central issues in evangelism from a cultural and biblical perspective. He hopes to stimulate fresh thinking on the whole subject of how we think about and practise evangelism.

David has written Part 2, 'Evangelism and the local church'. He writes from a wealth of experience in evangelism and pioneering new forms of church, and suggests some practical ways of earthing the principles of biblical evangelism in the ongoing life of churches and Christian communities.

1

How did we get here and where are we going?

David Male

Before we get into the details of our present situation and reflect on how we may reinvigorate evangelism in the church, it is worth stepping back for a moment and obtaining a wider historical perspective. I want to put before you five historical snapshots covering the last 100 years, which might shed some light on how we have arrived at the place where we are. If we can understand what has gone before, we may be in a better place to progress into the future without repeating the mistakes of the past.[2]

Snapshot 1: World Missionary Conference, Edinburgh, 1910

'The most notable gathering in the interest of the worldwide expansion of Christianity ever held, not only in missionary annals, but in all Christian annals.'[3] This was the huge claim made by John Mott, the Chairman of the first World Missionary Conference, held in Edinburgh just over 100 years ago. The conference celebrated all that had been happening in mission over the previous 50 years, but there was also a sense of prophetic intensity about the gathering. It was seen as a 'kairos' moment in the history of mission and even expressed the hope that the evangelisation of the world might be completed within a generation. The conference was addressed by the Archbishop of Canterbury, Randall Davidson, who declared, 'The place of missions in the life of the church must be the central place, and none other; that is what matters.'

The nationality of the delegates reveals much about the situation at the beginning of the 20th century. Around 1,200 delegates attended the conference, of whom over 1,000 came from either Britain or the USA. There were 18 delegates from Asia, none at all from Latin America and only one from Africa, and he was not a full delegate. How things would have changed by the end of the century! Philip Jenkins has summed it up superbly in his book *The Next Christendom*, 'Over the past century,' he writes, 'the center of gravity in the Christian world has shifted inexorably southward, to Africa and Latin America… Whatever Europeans or North Americans may believe, Christianity is doing very well indeed in the global south – not just surviving but expanding. This trend will continue apace in coming years.'[4]

The 1910 Conference, which was such a critical gathering, highlights two important issues for our present situation. The first is the danger of imperialism. Some of the missionary language of 'crusade' and 'campaign' continued into the rest of the century and has left the contemporary church feeling increasingly uncomfortable about evangelism, which it feels is about forcing people to do what they don't really want to do. This has combined with a radical pluralism which proclaims that no one faith can claim itself to be true above others. Matters of faith should be kept private and there should be no place for any activity that looks like proselytism.

Secondly, it reminds us that God does not serve our strategies but that our strategies must serve him. The outbreak of World War I was soon to change the high hopes of the Edinburgh conference. Often God works in ways that we do not foresee and cannot predict. The great news is that much of the hoped-for church growth has indeed happened, but not as a result of the western nations taking the gospel abroad; it has come about through the Africans, Latin Americans and Asians evangelising their own nations. Of course, the missionaries played a vital role in laying foundations for the later phenomenal growth but the evangelising has been done mostly by local people. Some amazing church growth has taken place recently in China, although western missionaries had been forced out of the country by 1953. Now, many nations from the global south are not only evangelising their own countries but are aiming to take the gospel to other parts of the world as well. My brother-in-law, who works with churches in South-East Asia, is presently in Latin America, advising local Christians who feel called by God to take the gospel to parts of Asia where the church is struggling.

The nations at the 1910 Missionary Conference that were confidently presenting their evangelistic credentials are now the areas needing most help. The church in such places is, by and large, in rapid decline and no longer at the centre of evangelisation of the world. This requires not just humility when facing the future but a recognition of the need to learn from Christians around the world. We are no longer the experts. Many sisters and brothers in Africa have been sharing the gospel in multifaith environments for many years, and will bring helpful lessons that apply to our situation. We need to remind ourselves that the church and evangelism are global enterprises with an outlet in most cities, towns and villages of this world. The churches' reach is greater than that of any of the major global brands. We are not part of a declining belief system but part of a worldwide vibrant faith, where God is at work.

Snapshot 2: 'Towards the Conversion of England', 1945

In 1945 a report by the Commission on Evangelism appointed by the Archbishops of York and Canterbury was released.[5] The original request, by the Church of England Assembly in 1943, asked the commission to 'survey the whole problem of modern evangelism, with special reference to the spiritual needs and prevailing intellectual outlook of the non-worshipping members of the community',[6] and to report on the organisation and methods by which such needs could most effectively be addressed.

To read the report today is to understand how little has changed over the decades. The opening chapter speaks of 'the wide and deep gulf between the Church and the people'.[7] It suggests that there is 'a wholesale drift from organised religion' and talks about 'the present irrelevance of the church in the life and thought of the community'. The authors continue, 'The obvious fact of the decline in church-going throws into high relief the need for finding new means whereby a hearing may be gained for the Gospel message.'[8]

In the conclusion, the authors suggested that 'for effective evangelism there is need not only to recover the apostolate of the whole Church, but also the fellowship of the Church'.[9]

These two elements were seen as key to the whole report. The first was the recognition that evangelism was for the whole church: it needed everyone to be involved, not just a self-selecting few. As part of life in Christ, every Christian was sent into the world to witness to and for Christ. Today the church is still hampered by the viewpoint that evangelism is for the few who are 'into that kind of thing'. The report commented that 'the mobilisation of the laity for the work of evangelism is in the very forefront of our Recommendations' and that 'England will never be converted until the laity use the opportunities for evangelism daily afforded'.[10] This has to be the work of everyone in the church, working together, rather than being the special interest of a small group. The 'Imagine' project[11] run by the London Institute for Contemporary Christianity (LICC) has provided some rich research in this area through its 'What the People Said' survey of 2003. This showed that even the most committed Christians felt ill-equipped to share their faith and that a 'pastor-centric' model of church actively inhibits the equipping of the whole congregation for mission. There was also a strong sense that congregational members received no help in bridging the gap between their church attendance and the rest of their lives.

Second, the report emphasised the importance of discipleship. When Archbishop William Temple addressed the first meeting of the commission, he spoke about the need for a quickening of spiritual life within the church: 'We cannot separate the evangelisation of those without from the rekindling of devotion from within.'[12] The report itself talked about the church being 'half converted', and about the need for people in society to see the change that conversion brings to the life of the church community. It concluded by quoting words from a conference on evangelism held in Jerusalem in 1924:

> The only spiritual dynamic is the Living Spirit of the Crucified and Risen Christ himself. The whole… world is awaiting the release of this vital force through human personalities, vitalised by the Holy Spirit, and witnessing with a new power to the Cross of Christ as the central fact of faith and life. We submit that the spiritual dynamic for such a compelling witness is, in the good purpose of God always available.[13]

In more recent times, the 'Imagine' research undertaken by LICC has come to similar conclusions. Its authors reported that their research 'convinced us that the missional issue of the evangelisation of the UK is essentially a discipleship issue. The UK will not be won for Christ by discovering a silver bullet or by seeing people come into an institution that they distrust but by equipping God's people to live well wherever they are'.[14] We will return to this vital issue in chapter 10, but it highlights the need for the church itself to be changed in order to be in a position to change the world.

So why did the Commission on Evangelism's report at the end of World War II not change the life of the church? Unfortunately, just after the report was published, Archbishop William Temple died and his successors began to concentrate on the reformation of Canon

Law and the liturgy of the church rather than the evangelisation of the nation. This highlights the continuing challenge for the institution of the church not simply to keep the show going but to reform and adapt itself so as to reconnect with the majority of the population. Practically, much of this reconnection will need to be done at the local level, but central institutions and denominations can set the tone and strategy as well as providing encouragement, support and resources for evangelism.

Snapshot 3: Billy Graham's first visit to Britain, 1954

It is estimated that more than 1.75 million people heard Billy Graham preaching over a period of twelve weeks during his first ever visit to the UK in 1954. Most of the evening events were held in London's Harringay Arena but the final event was conducted at Wembley Stadium. This single gathering holds the record for the largest ever crowd at the Old Wembley Stadium, with 120,000 people packed into the venue itself, and a further 67,000 in the overflow at White City Stadium. Prime Minister Winston Churchill invited Billy Graham to 10 Downing Street, and Graham preached for the Queen at Windsor Castle. Although initially sceptical, the national press claimed that a revival was taking place and that this was a good thing.

In many ways, this was the high point for a type of large-scale evangelism that had become the norm for many years in the church. It was based largely upon the revivalist models developed by earlier American evangelists such as Charles Finney, D.L. Moody and Billy Sunday. Its final flourish in Britain was probably 'Mission England' in 1984, when Billy Graham used a number of football grounds around the UK to preach the gospel.

This type of evangelism was replicated (and still is in some places) at a local level, with many churches holding gospel events, guest services and regular mission weeks. Often a well-known itinerant evangelist would be recruited to give the evangelistic talks. Usually, as in the large townwide meetings, people would be invited to come to the front at the end of the event to pray a prayer of commitment.

The legacy of this model for the church was that evangelism came to be equated with putting on a large-scale mission with evangelistic preaching. There were many benefits to this model, and many people became Christians through it, but it also had its drawbacks. One of the main problems was the sheer effort involved. A big mission could take two years to organise (and then another two years for the church people to recover from it). Many asked if all this energy was best used for one week of intense evangelistic activity. Some people felt that it was manipulative, as the large meetings swayed people's emotions, or that the personality of the preacher became too important. Others felt that it severed the link between evangelism and the local church.

Nonetheless, this form of evangelism, with its call to conversion, worked well for people who had a good basic grasp of the Christian story, and many found that their faith was ignited by it. But for a more uninformed, sceptical, postmodern audience, the idea of being lectured from the front by an expert is seen as old-fashioned and past its sell-by date. At the start of the 20th century, about 80% of people in the UK had contact with the church (not least through its Sunday schools or youth groups), but by the end of the century this figure had fallen to a mere twelve per cent. George Barna, in his book on evangelism, sums up the issue:

> To be honest, the environment in which we live is not even like the one in which Billy Graham ministered so powerfully and remarkably. We cannot be effective if we continue to cling to the old ways, the old strategies, the old assumptions. We do not live in that era, and we cannot be effective if we behave in a manner relevant only to the past.[15]

There has been a significant shift in thinking about evangelism from the dominant 'crisis model', where people were expected to leave their seats to make a commitment at a meeting or service, to a 'process model', which recognises that there is nearly always a much longer and more complex route involved in someone's decision to become a follower of Jesus. This process might include a number of elements: getting to know a Christian, maybe attending church meetings over a period of time, reading some Christian literature and attending a small group to discover more about faith. In John Finney's research 20 years ago, studying 500 people with little church background who had become Christians over a twelve-month period, he discovered that it was rarely a single event that led to faith but a gradual shift over time, particularly dependent on relationships with Christians. He wrote that the 'gradual process is the way in which the majority of people discover God and the average time taken is about four years: models of evangelism which can help people along the pathway are needed'.[16]

The shift away from a large-scale mission model has made many church leaders feel nervous. We may not like the big crusade model, but we have very little with which to replace it. Some churches have continued with a regular programme of guest services and mission weeks but have generally found that fewer and fewer non-Christians are attending them. (This has also begged the question as to what an evangelist actually *is* if he or she is not standing at the front preaching evangelistically at large meetings.)

I think there is still a place for this model in evangelism, and we do not help ourselves if we simply abandon it, but it needs to be one among many. In his survey of contemporary evangelistic methods, Mike Booker comments, 'The residual faith that enabled one single, eloquent appeal to make such an impact is generally no longer present… The expectations of some clergy and church members may be still coloured by their own experiences of crusade evangelism.' He goes on to say, 'There may well still be important ways in which parish missions and travelling evangelists can fit into local church evangelistic strategies today, but it is only honest first to face up to some of the disappointments generated by special mission events.'[17] The problem it caused was that, for many years, evangelism was equated only with this model – if you wanted to do evangelism, you put on a mission – but an evangelistic course from a church in London was to change this dynamic irrevocably.

Snapshot 4: The rise of Alpha, 1990

The ten-week 'Basics Course' for new believers at Holy Trinity Brompton, first created by Charles Marnham, was developed by John Irvine and then by Nicky Gumbel to appeal to people outside the church.[18] It has since become a worldwide phenomenon running in over 100 countries and over 100 languages, with over 24 million people having taken the course. There are now Alpha courses for students, youth, seniors, prisons, workplaces and the armed forces.

The Alpha course did more than provide an excellent evangelistic opportunity; it has had a huge influence on the churches' understanding of and approach to evangelism. It has probably been the most significant single reason why people now regard evangelism as a longer-term process, based on a Christian's individual relationships with friends outside the church. It pioneered many elements of evangelism that we assume now to be the norm, such as giving people time and space to learn about Christianity, and setting evangelism in a relaxed and informal environment. It also highlighted the importance of giving people the opportunity to ask questions and engage in discussion rather than listening to a speaker at the front. Finally, it showed the important role that food and eating together play in developing good relationships and providing a conducive environment in which to learn and grow. Many other similar courses have developed, following the success of Alpha. Although they may differ in some of their content, the basic model is very similar: a course over a number of weeks, including a talk on a specific key subject, small group discussion, freedom to explore and ask questions, all within the setting of a shared meal.

John Finney suggests a number of reasons why such groups work. They are built around relationships; they are relaxed but have a goal; they are group-based but church linked; they do not dictate how people find God, yet they create space for people to do so; they blend reason and experience; they are often lay-led, and they give room for the Holy Spirit to work.[19] These courses have, in some senses, taken over the role of the evangelist, and have certainly helped the church to realise that the process of coming to faith usually takes time. (It needs to be added, of course, that there is often a sudden experience – or experiences – within the process.)

Much of the success of courses such as Alpha is that they reignite a childhood faith. Alpha itself began its life as a kind of Confirmation course and assumes some degree of understanding of the Christian faith. The 'European Values Study' of 2010 (a large-scale longitudinal survey research programme) clearly showed the link between childhood attendance at church and the possibility of future faith. It concluded that 94% of current churchgoers attended church at least occasionally at the age of around 11 or 12. But one of the problems we face is that childhood church attendance is in rapid decline. The Church of England's own figures suggest that the number of children attending church on a Sunday fell by 42% between 1989 and 2005.

The problem for the future of courses like Alpha is that the number of people with background knowledge is shrinking dramatically. Churches are beginning to discover that any materials they use need to start much further back. When we planted a church in Huddersfield called 'The Net',[20] we used Alpha as a course for people once they had become Christians. For those at the investigative stage, we needed something much more basic, so we wrote our own course based on Luke's gospel. The sociologist Stephen Hunt comments that 'Alpha has impacted UK churches and thousands worldwide on an impressive scale', but he says of those attending that 'the greater contingent is already in the church and constitutes committed Christians, although there is a sense in which Alpha brings in those on the fringes of the church – perhaps those who attend infrequently or only on special occasions'.[21] This is not a criticism of a great course but it does highlight the changing situation of a population with less and less church experience and Christian knowledge.

In exploring the changing face of evangelism, John Finney has examined the role of courses in evangelism today. He suggests that their downside is that they are somewhat artificial, they only attract the curious and extrovert, and they suit the educated and articulate. He also notes that much of the content is set by the course rather than the agenda of the participants.[22] Finney concludes, 'Enthusiast though I am, I have to admit the nurture group is not the answer for everyone.'[23] Tellingly, Mark Ireland, in a book evaluating many of the present evangelistic courses, comments:

> The main problem at the moment appears not to be the lack of evangelism courses, but the lack of people to go on them, which suggests churches need to do significant preparatory work in which enquirers set their own agenda and raise their own questions before many of them are ready to work through somebody else's agenda in a published course.[24]

We may need to think more radically about the nature of the process of evangelism in order to connect with those who have very little understanding or interest in the gospel. It is fascinating to see developments like the 'Table Talk' course, which is aimed at people at a much earlier stage of their spiritual journey.[25] Its website recognises the changing situation and comments that 'there are incredible opportunities for sharing our faith, but the old ways of outworking the Great Commission, individually and corporately, don't work as well with most of the tribes in these new lands'. One of the main problems is that we no longer have a 'shared spiritual vocabulary' with which to talk about the gospel and Christian faith. This is highlighted in our final snapshot.

Snapshot 5: The rise of Stormzy, 2018

Stormzy, the stage name of London-born grime artist Michael Omari, has undoubtedly taken the music world by storm recently. He initially rose to fame through his recordings on YouTube, but his celebrity really took off with the release of his debut album, *Gang Signs and Prayers*, which went straight to number one. He has won various music awards, including British Male Solo Artist at the 2018 BRIT Awards. In a recent interview, Stormzy said, 'I 100 per cent believe in God – it's a very important thing in my life. I'm lucky to be where I am now with my career. I hustled and struggled, then everything just happened at the right time. It was all God's timing, but my work. God, my family and being real are the most important things to me. Everything else comes second.'[26]

Gang Signs and Prayers highlights some of the controversy surrounding him. One of the songs, 'Blinded by Grace', contains lyrics that would not be out of place in a modern worship song, touching on the themes of our brokenness and God's gracious salvation. But the album also contains lyrics about revenge and drug taking and contains many swear words. There has been much debate over whether he is putting his faith into action, as his lyrics express the reality of betrayal, family breakdown and depression, or whether there is a lack of consistency in his faith. Whatever the case, he voices for many young people their deepest feelings, aspirations and concerns.

Stormzy's story leads me to wonder how many of our churches could cope with someone like him – not because of his celebrity lifestyle but because of his background and vocabulary of faith. The church in general is often more inclined to connect with a particular type of person. But what about the young men and women who are much more likely to be found in a nightclub than a church? Stormzy didn't always talk about his faith in a conventional religious way. How do we help people find a vocabulary for their spiritual journey and their experiences of Jesus? Many missionaries, when they go overseas, spend their first two years not doing conventional missionary work but simply learning the local language. Maybe, in many parts of our society, that is where the church needs to start again, simply learning the local language. Perhaps in time we would become able to communicate the unchanging truths of the gospel more effectively.

Church too easily becomes a self-contained community that speaks only to itself and so gives up its role of communicating the gospel in a language that can be understood by a greater part of society. John Stackhouse from Regent College, Vancouver, talks about the need to 'distil the gospel', by which he means the requirement for Christians to understand it deeply, live it and learn how to speak it within our church communities. Having done this deep work of understanding, we may be better able to communicate it clearly and confidently in our neighbour's language.[27]

When I was newly ordained, I was asked to lead a Communion service at Leicester Cathedral. I was very nervous, despite the fact that the service was at 8am on a Tuesday morning with a congregation of six (including me). I confess that I led the service poorly. At the end, the verger took me into a small room to get changed. He told me that he was going off for breakfast and said, 'Just come back out of this door and it will lock behind you.' I think I had been flustered by the whole experience, so, instead of coming out of that door, I went through another one, which led me into what I can only describe as a large cupboard. I thought this would be fine, as I would just return to the first room and then go out the way the verger had described. Unfortunately, when I tried to do so, I discovered that this door had locked behind me and I was trapped in the small room.

This was before mobile phones and I did not want to have to wait until I was discovered later in the day. I looked around and saw a small gap at knee level in a huge, thick, wooden door. The door would not open but, when I looked through the hole, I realised that it was adjacent to a path running alongside the cathedral. As I looked through, I could see people hurrying to work. I waited until people were near enough and shouted through the hole as loudly as

I could, 'Can you help me? I am locked in the cathedral!' Eventually someone kindly stopped and came over to the gap, and I explained my predicament. I asked if they could go over to the Cathedral Office and enquire if someone could come and release me. Sure enough, within five minutes I was let out – much to the amusement of the entire cathedral staff.

My embarrassing story provides a picture of the experience of the church. There is a real danger that we will only communicate within our church communities. When we occasionally shout out to those outside, we wonder why they run past us so quickly. We need to be breaking down the barriers, connecting and communicating with the people around us. I see churches that are good at making connections in their communities but struggle to articulate their faith in Jesus. I also meet churches that are wonderful at articulating their faith and spend much time polishing their words, but they have very few connections in their communities so they don't have anyone outside the church to communicate the words to!

But I also see real signs of hope as I travel around the world observing what God is doing in and through his church. I notice three particular things happening, which might suggest some of the directions we will be taking in the future.

First, I see a church seeking to re-engage with society, to break out, connecting and communicating with their local communities. I now meet many more church leaders who recognise the fact that we are not connecting with those outside the church. The old refill factor is no longer in operation. A new generation of people does not come into church to replace those who are leaving or dying. I have seen churches using initiatives like the Street Pastors scheme,[28] or prayers for healing on the streets, all of which aim to get the church out into the neighbourhood.[29] In Cambridge, some local church leaders regularly take a sofa into the local shopping area and offer a space for people to talk with them about anything they like. One of my friends, Chris Duffett, has done some amazingly imaginative evangelistic work on the streets of Peterborough, among other places, for example, by creating pieces of art on the theme of 'faith'.[30]

Second, I see a re-imagination of what church is and might become. In many places, I hear about Messy Church, 'surfing church', 'coffee church', 'sports church', 'film church' and many other forms of church. I recently heard about two examples of 'knitting churches'. One was in the north of England and had developed out of a meeting called 'Knit and Natter'. Then I heard about a knitting church in London, which was full of young people because (as I discovered recently) knitting is becoming very much in vogue for those in their 20s. Such stories make us ask some really important questions about what church is and what it does, and they may lead us into some exciting places as we seek to get the word out.

Finally, there seems to be a reorientation to whole-life discipleship. It is exciting to see developments in churches such as missional communities, new monasticism and mission-shaped discipleship.[31] We are realising that discipleship is not simply measured by church attendance but is related to the whole of our lives.

These are strong shoots of hope, which we must nourish and which give us some important pointers to our future direction.

Questions

- How has the perception of evangelism changed in your congregation over the last ten years?

- What do you think is the dominant model of evangelism that your church is working from?

- In what ways might the practice of evangelism look different in ten years' time?

2

A walk in the neighbourhood: evangelism and our culture

Paul Weston

David Male and I are both based in the city of Cambridge. It is a remarkable and world-famous city, full of ancient buildings of great significance and architectural beauty. I sometimes ask my students to imagine a Martian spaceship landing on the front lawn of the college where we teach. The door opens and an intergalactic visitor makes her way tentatively down the steps and asks for a quick tour around the city. Her only request is that you point out its most significant buildings and explain their significance. How long, I ask, do you think it would be before you had to explain the Christian story?

Not long, I suspect. As you walked towards the city centre, you'd cross Silver Street bridge and point out the slim tall tower built into the street edge of Queens' College, which has come to be known as the 'Erasmus' tower. Here, Desiderius Erasmus, the Renaissance scholar, worked on critical editions of the Latin and Greek texts of the New Testament between 1510 and 1515, both of which provided significant impetus for the beginnings of the English Reformation.

In under a minute, you'd be at the junction of Silver Street with Trumpington Street, pointing out St Botolph's Church just opposite, whose main tower dates back to the mid-14th century and which has been a centre of Christian worship for longer still. Turning left towards the centre, you'd pass Corpus Christi College on your right, where the Front Court was rebuilt in the early 19th century to emphasise the presence of the chapel, the first thing you see through the opening archway. Then, beyond Corpus Christi, you'd turn right (noting the blue plaque outside the Eagle pub where, to a bemused audience of drinkers, Francis Crick and James Watson announced the discovery of the DNA molecule in 1953), and point out the tower of St Bene't's Church, which dates back to the Anglo-Saxon period just before the invasion of William the Conqueror in 1066, and is the oldest standing building in Cambridgeshire. Then you would come to perhaps the most iconic sight of all in central Cambridge: the south face of King's Chapel, which was begun in the middle of the 15th century and took nearly 100 years to complete – and so on. By this stage, you would only have walked about 600 metres, but it would have been impossible to do so without recounting to your Martian visitor the profound impact that the Christian story has had upon the life of the city.

Cambridge is somewhat unusual, of course, but in concentrated form it reflects a more general characteristic of British culture. Our architectural landscape is still Christian – whether it be the church towers or steeples presiding over countless towns and villages or the vast cathedrals that continue to tower over our cityscapes – yet our intellectual landscape is now increasingly post-Christian. We are still surrounded by Christian buildings but their significance is no longer mainstream. For some time now, our thinking has been more decisively influenced by other cultural forces. Our architecture may still be Christian but our mindset is no longer so.

Two words have come to be associated with this cultural transition, and they each help to describe the nature of the momentous changes that have been taking place within western culture. Both

need to be thought about carefully as we consider their implications for evangelism. The first is 'secularisation' and the second is
'postmodernity'.

Contemporary western culture is 'secular'

'Secularisation' is one of those buzzwords that have spawned a set
of seemingly cast-iron assumptions about contemporary culture.
Broadly defined, it describes the removal of religious significance
from the structures and processes of cultural life. As Os Guinness
has put it, secularisation is 'the process through which, starting from
the centre and moving outwards, successive sectors of society and
culture have been freed from the decisive influence of religious ideas
and institutions'.[32]

At one level, this is clearly true. As was noted in the previous
chapter, 20th-century churchgoing figures underwent what Steve
Bruce describes as a 'remorseless decline relative to the adult
population'.[33] The 2007 Tearfund report entitled *Churchgoing in the
UK* estimated that two-thirds of the adult population now have no
connection whatever with church, and that 'churchgoing is simply
not on their agenda'. 'The secular majority,' it says, 'presents a major
challenge to churches.'[34]

This situation means that we need to think harder about how we
communicate the good news of Jesus in our contemporary world.
There are two reasons for this.

First, the rapid decline in church membership over the last 50 years
means that the religious and biblical vocabulary we once used is
no longer current among today's population. Twenty years ago, the
Church of England's report entitled *All God's Children?* indicated that
in 1955, 83 per cent of adults who tuned in to the 'Daily Service' on
the radio had attended some form of Sunday school or Bible class
for several years in their childhood.[35] Even if this figure is drastically

reduced owing to the unrepresentative nature of the sample, it still suggests that two-thirds of the adult population in the 1930s and 1940s regularly attended some sort of organised Sunday school. By contrast, the 1989 *English Church Census* showed that only 14% of children under the age of 15 participated in any form of church-related activity on Sundays.[36] In the Church of England in 1979, the single largest group by percentage was the under-15s. By the close of the millennium, it was the over-65s.[37]

Christian vocabulary that meant something in previous generations no longer resonates in the way it once did. I well remember giving a talk on 'The evidence for the resurrection' at a student bar meeting in a prestigious British university and being thanked afterwards by a history student, who said he had come along for the simple reason that he had never heard of 'the resurrection' and wanted to know what it was. But this ignorance doesn't relate just to individual words like 'sin' or 'salvation', but to the wider 'webs' of meaning in which these words properly operate. These webs, which were once held together both by the widespread practice of church attendance and its accompanying working knowledge of religious language, are now dissolving rapidly. As a result, our religious language is often marooned, lacking the cultural anchors that it once had.

Second, the process of secularisation plays into a broader set of assumptions that affect both Christians and non-Christians. At their heart, these assumptions interpret Christian faith as passé. The remarkable church architecture of Cambridge and elsewhere clearly communicates that Christian faith meant something once, but the relevance of the church is now consigned to the past. It may be part of our heritage but has little to do with the present. Church buildings are therefore best categorised alongside museums as places of historical interest with little relevance to the here and now. Subconsciously, this assumption creates psychological barriers to Christian witness, as if we are already on a losing wicket, and it makes the job of evangelism – hard as it is already – harder still.

Secularisation rules?

Although the process of secularisation is so commonly accepted in the current climate of the west, it is worth exploring what it means in a little more detail.

Stemming from the sociological circles of the 1960s, the theory of secularisation owed many of its roots to the late flowering of 'modernity', the cultural era spawned by the Enlightenment of the 17th and 18th centuries. A prevailing assumption of modernity was that, with the progress of science and technology, the space for religious belief was diminishing. As Max Planck, the father of quantum physics, wrote in his *Autobiography* published in 1950, 'faith in miracles must yield ground, step by step, before the steady and firm advance of the forces of science, and its total defeat is indubitably a mere matter of time'.[38] As a result, the American sociologist Peter Berger (an early believer in the theory of secularisation) wrote in the *New York Times* in 1968, 'By the 21st century, religious believers are likely to be found only in small sects, huddled together to resist a worldwide secular culture.'[39]

However, it is worth noting that people had already been forecasting the end of religion for over 300 years, without success. English theologian Thomas Woolston, for example, had confidently predicted in 1710 that Christianity would have disappeared altogether by the end of the 19th century. Fifty years after this prediction, the great French philosopher Voltaire came to the conclusion that Woolston had been rather too cautious in his forecast, and wrote to Frederick the Great explaining that Woolston could not possibly have taken more recent events into consideration. If he had, he would have seen that religion 'is crumbling of itself, and its fall will be but the more rapid'.[40] With the benefit of hindsight, we can see that neither Woolston nor Voltaire got it right. Indeed, within 100 years of Voltaire's comments, Christianity was to flower in Britain and experience substantial growth in the late Victorian era, to say nothing of the expansion of Christianity worldwide in the years since.

How has the newer 1960s theory of secularisation fared? Interestingly, this too has come in for some rather drastic revisions. Peter Berger is one of a number of proponents of the original theory who has had to change his mind in the light of more recent evidence. Writing in 1999, he wrote that 'the assumption that we live in a secularised world is false. The world today, with some exceptions… is as furiously religious as it ever was, and in some places more so than ever.'[41] In the light of this, he – along with a number of others – more commonly refer nowadays to theories of '*de*-secularisation'.

These newer approaches – while not denying aspects of the original thesis – have emphasised the complexity of the secularisation process. For example, sociologists such as Karel Dobbelaere and José Casanova have shown that it develops differently in the public and institutional dimensions of culture than in the spheres of private belief and behaviour. The original theory had tended to 'flatline' these processes, as if they were one and the same thing, assuming that, as public and institutional life became increasingly secularised, private individuals would cease to believe. But this is being increasingly questioned, especially in western Europe. Writers such as Grace Davie have shown that it is not so much that individuals have ceased to believe, but that belief has become increasingly disassociated from membership of religious institutions and church congregations. The marked fall-off rate in church attendance is not necessarily purely a sign of declining belief, but is part of a wider cultural phenomenon of institutional dislocation. Accordingly, Davie wrote in 1994, 'The overall pattern of religious life is changing. For it appears that more and more people within British society want to believe but do not want to involve themselves in religious practice.' She subtitled the book from which this quotation is taken 'Believing without belonging'.[42]

Secularisation and evangelism

What are the implications of this revised approach as we think about evangelism? As noted earlier, one of the subtle effects of 'secularisation-speak' is that it breeds something of a defeatist attitude among Christians. 'What is the point of evangelising if it is clear that we are fighting a losing battle?' The assumptions we bring to a task – whether they be openly expressed or subconsciously felt – are highly significant for the way we approach that task, so I suggest that there are at least two things we need to bear in mind.

The first, as we have seen, is that history demonstrates that the processes of secularisation are neither inevitable nor predictable. We need to remind ourselves repeatedly that the challenges facing us are no different in kind to those that the church faced in previous generations.

The second thing to bear in mind as we think about secularisation is that what Professor Rodney Stark has called the 'supply-side' of faith is not in decline at all. Although some leading thinkers continue to say that the religious 'instinct' will be extinguished, this has proved to be far from true. Indeed, as Richard Middleton and Brian Walsh have commented, 'Far from the erosion or even eclipse of religious belief that the Enlightenment so confidently predicted, the Enlightenment itself has been eclipsed, resulting in a veritable smorgasbord of religions and worldviews for our consumption.'[43]

Despite the talk of secularisation, therefore, we need to remember that we are not speaking into a culture where the concept of faith is absent – far from it. The New Testament authors assume more readily than we do that there is a religious dimension to cultural life in all its forms, and that faith is habitually being expressed, even if in ways that are not immediately identified or acknowledged. At Athens, for example, the apostle Paul starts his speech at the Areopagus by noting 'how extremely religious you are in every way' (Acts 17:22). We will look at this speech in more detail in chapter 5, but I simply want to say at this point that Paul's main intention is not to manufacture faith where there is none, but rather to redirect existing faith towards its proper goal: 'What therefore you worship as unknown, this I proclaim to you' (v. 23).

This assumption puts a rather different spin on the barriers in our so-called 'secularised' culture. Indeed, some social commentators are starting to question the value of the word 'secular' itself. Grace Davie, for example, wrote in the early 1990s, 'We do not live in a secular society. We live in a society in which belief is drifting away from orthodoxy to no one knows where; in which belief is floating, disconnected without an anchor.'[44] Missionary theologian Lesslie Newbigin always preferred to describe western culture as 'pagan' rather than 'secular' for this very reason. He wrote, 'We have learned, I think, that what has come into being is not a secular society but a pagan society, not a society devoid of public images but a society which worships gods which are not God.'[45]

This way of reinterpreting the 'secular' nature of our western culture may thus help to equip rather than hinder us in our evangelism. Rather than thinking that we are attempting to bring something completely new into the lives of our friends, perhaps we should consider evangelism more in terms of redirecting their worship.

Postmodernity

Alongside the processes of secularisation, the sweep of cultural change loosely described as 'postmodernity' has served to diversify and dilute the structures of classical Christian belief.

As John Drane put it nearly 20 years ago, 'When people of 2020 look back to the 1980s and 1990s, I believe they will see that we have been in the middle of a paradigm shift as significant as those inaugurated in the past by Copernicus, Newton or Einstein.'[46] This is a big claim, but it is borne out by the rapid social changes in belief and attitude. A central feature of the newer postmodern landscape is the suspicion of what writers have come to describe as modern 'metanarratives'. A metanarrative can be defined as the attempt to encompass the meaning of human existence in a single narrative or story. As Jean-François Lyotard, one of the most influential of postmodern thinkers, famously wrote, 'Simplifying to the extreme, I define *postmodern* as incredulity toward metanarratives.'[47] Postmodernity, as Terry Eagleton says, 'is a style of thought which is suspicious of classical notions of truth, reason, identity and objectivity, of the idea of universal progress or emancipation, of single frameworks, grand narratives or ultimate grounds of explanation.'[48]

The 20th century spawned quite a few metanarratives. There was the one about western imperialism (with its spread of the Enlightenment ideals of progress and rationalism); there was the one developed by Karl Marx (with its unifying theories about class and society); and there was, of course, the Nazi myth (with its particularly sinister beliefs about racial superiority and domination). But the transition to postmodernity has relativised these older grand or 'meta' narratives and, in the process, has set out to liberate a range of other stories that had been marginalised, so that they too can be heard. Above all, postmodernity will no longer allow the presumption that any single story can be understood as definitive – however 'enlightened' it might appear.

Of course, it isn't just the 20th-century narratives that have come under suspicion from the postmoderns. Christianity itself is a metanarrative *par excellence*, explaining human origins, indicating human destiny and demonstrating for all time that the meaning of human existence is to be found in the person of Jesus Christ. One of the challenges to contemporary evangelism, therefore, is that Christianity has come under the same suspicion as other grand narratives, and for the same reasons.

This postmodern way of seeing things cuts two ways for the would-be evangelist. It recognises that any personal worldview is a valid belief-option (and therefore gives Christianity the right to be heard), but it doesn't allow any such worldview to be more than a personal one. Christians cannot, therefore, seek to win anybody to their view of reality on the basis that it is more true than other views. They certainly cannot claim that their view is uniquely and universally true.

In responding to this sort of scenario, some Christian apologists want to accept that, since we have now moved into a postmodern era, we can no longer say that the gospel is 'true' in the sense that we once did. All we can do is to pitch our faith in the public arena as one truth among many and hope for the best. In one sense, you could say that this is an improvement over modernity, where religious accounts of reality were often dismissed altogether, but it comes with a heavy price: Christianity may be true for you, but you cannot say that it is true for everyone.

Responding to cultural change

Along with the idea of secularisation, the laid-back and slightly chaotic pluralism of postmodernity presents an acute challenge to traditional forms of Christian communication. The ways in which we communicate the message may fall under suspicion before any of the content of the Christian message is even heard. So how do we understand evangelism in these circumstances, and how do we go about doing it?

That, of course, is the subject of the book as a whole, and we will be exploring various aspects in the chapters that follow. But in this introductory discussion on the impact of culture on understandings of evangelism, it is worth setting the discussion in the wider context of how the bigger ideas of 'gospel' and 'culture' have been understood to relate to one another. For example, do cultural assumptions have such an impact upon the way that we think that, in the end, its presuppositions must subtly determine the way in which we evangelise? Might this actually be a good thing, making the good news more 'relevant' to the people we are trying to reach? Or should the gospel set the agenda for our methodologies of apologetics and evangelism? And if this is the case, what kind of difference would it make in practice?

As a way of thinking through some of these questions, I have often used the framework set out by Peter Berger in his book *The Heretical Imperative*.[49] Here he looks in some detail at the impact of secularising cultures upon Christian communities and explores how Christians adapt to the challenges that they pose in terms of communicating religious faith. In particular, he looks at three possible ways in which religious faith can be affirmed in a culture in which it is being challenged.

The reductive option ('Going with the flow')

One characteristic response places 'relevance' as the highest priority. After all, if we are not heard by those around us as saying something that connects with their lives, what is the point of evangelism? Surely the good news must be relevant to them.

The problem with this type of approach, says Berger, is that it can easily become 'reductive'. It is marked, he says, by 'an exchange of authorities: the authority of modern thought or con- sciousness is substituted for the authority of the tradition… Modern consciousness and its alleged categories become the only criteria of validity for religious reflection.'[50] In other words, under this response to cultural change, you end up only saying things that tick the 'relevance' box.

Berger uses Rudolf Bultmann's demythologising programme of the 1950s as an example of what happens when the 'cognitive bargaining' process between traditional religious belief and con- temporary culture is determined by what hearers are prepared to accept. Bultmann argued that when aspects of the Christian faith become culturally unacceptable, they must either be jettisoned completely or radically reformulated so that they continue to make sense. He argued that some very central events of the faith (for example, the atonement, resurrection and ascension) were originally depicted in mythological ways. If Christianity continued to depend upon these methods in its proclamation, then it was finished, because 'modern man' could no longer believe in such fantasies.[51]

We may instinctively disagree with Bultmann's approach, but we should perhaps pause to acknowledge that much contemporary evangelism is in danger of falling into an essentially similar trap. We cannot say more than our friends and neighbours are willing to accept. Our surrounding culture dictates what may be said about Jesus Christ. Actually, in the light of what we have seen about postmodernity, this may mean we are able to say more than we could a generation ago. For example, we can speak of Jesus as a spiritual 'presence' or as an unseen companion. We can even talk of praying to him. But if we are ultimately constrained by cultural assumptions, it is out of the question to speak, for example, of Jesus as the unique and only revelation of God, and to say that people need to be forgiven. If we allow the reductive tendency to dictate what we say in our evangelism, the gospel cloth – in a manner rather uncomfortably similar to that of Bultmann – is subtly recut to fit the cultural suit.

The inductive option ('Fanning any faith flame!')

Berger's second way of responding to cultural change is described as 'inductive'. Whereas the reductive approach still wants in some sense to maintain the validity of the Christian message, but sees that the only way to do so is to adapt it to the surrounding culture, the 'inductive' approach abandons any idea of a particular belief-system that is more important than any other. The important thing is not the tradition in which faith occurs but the phenomenon of faith itself. So the essence of the inductive approach 'is to turn to experience as the ground of all religious affirmations – one's own experience to whatever extent this is possible, and the experience embodied in a particular range of traditions'.[52] Faith becomes extracted from particular belief-systems, whether Christian, Hindu, Buddhist or whatever. Faith is what we want to share, and it doesn't really matter where it comes from.

In a culture of increased religious pluralism, this becomes a very attractive approach. We stress faith itself as the important thing – in whatever form it takes – and avoid any insistence upon particular traditions of belief such as Christianity. Berger realises that this will be a real challenge to Christians. It will involve 'a re-evaluation of the Christian tradition from an inductive viewpoint "to uncover the experiential substrata of the tradition". This must be done in relation to itself and also to other religious traditions. There are risks in this programme, but never to *faith*. This is the way ahead.'[53] Such a route is already being commonly championed in our culture, not least within the educational establishment. Here, any expression of faith must be safeguarded and nurtured, while any form of proselytism or evangelism is rigorously avoided.

As with the reductive option, many Christians will understandably want to reject the assumptions behind the inductive approach. Before we move on, though, it's worth pausing to think about how these inductive assumptions – which have become so much a part of our cultural mindset – have influenced the way in which Christians think about evangelism. At one level, the cultural tendency towards what Berger calls the 'grounding of Christian faith' in 'religious experience' has had a clear impact on styles of evangelism. The emphasis on 'telling our stories' and 'giving our testimonies' is perhaps an example of this trend. For sure, the vitality of personal faith is at the very heart of effective outreach, and evangelism is all but dead without it. Particularly in the context of postmodernity, it represents a great way in to talking about our faith. But the question is: does our evangelism go any further than this? If it doesn't, are we not actually agreeing with the inductive approach? Some years ago, I overheard a person in a pub conversation with one of the members of a mission team that I was leading. 'It's great that you have found peace and fulfilment through your faith in Jesus,' he said. 'My own faith in _____ does the same for me.'

The scriptures never dismiss experience as unimportant for faith, but neither do they detach experience from the gospel events that made it possible. The objective and the experiential are held together. As the pub conversation shows, once Christian experience is divorced from the events that gave rise to it, it becomes very difficult to distinguish it from other manifestations of religious experience. This is exactly the kind of thing that Berger is talking about, so it's worth thinking about in relation to our own evangelism. It may be a brilliant starting point for evangelism but it cannot be all that we talk about.

The deductive option ('Keep doing what we've always done')

In sharp contrast to the reductive and inductive approaches, Berger's third way of responding to cultural change will instinctively appeal to those for whom 'faithfulness to the original gospel' is the paramount consideration. If our culture rejects Christianity, the 'deductive' response is to go on insisting that we proclaim 'the faith once delivered', whatever response we receive. In Berger's language, it is to 'reassert the authority of a religious tradition in the face of modern secularity'.[54]

Many readers will reject both the reductive and inductive approaches as flawed, and put most weight on the deductive category, for while both the reductive and the inductive options do not fit easily with the New Testament picture of the revelation of God in Jesus Christ as being his final word, the deductive option does. We do believe that in Jesus the world has seen God's final word. We do believe in a religious reality that is 'sovereignly independent' of any cultural setting. The deductive option appears rightly to maintain a commitment to the gospel as an objective revelation of truth, with its accompanying experience of God, while emphasising our continuing need to proclaim and defend it as such.

As with any set of models, there are inevitably elements of overlap between Berger's approaches. None of them is watertight or exclusive on its own. There is clearly a complex interplay between the 'gospel' and 'culture' (as Berger's categories demonstrate). But I want to make sure that the revelation of the gospel leads that interplay. This means allowing the revealed truth of Jesus to lead my thinking and practice about evangelism in changing cultural contexts. I therefore find myself most in sympathy with the deductive option.

However, I want to go on to ask: what does this mean in our contemporary culture, in terms of the content of our evangelism as well as the ways in which we seek to evangelise? There are dangers with the deductive approach, as there are with the others. As an example, Berger uses Karl Barth to illustrate the deductive approach. I'm a great admirer of Barth's theology but, while he was forthright about the 'otherness' of the gospel, he wasn't known for his ability (or desire) to be culturally adaptive. In some forms of contemporary evangelism, therefore, an unthinking deductive approach runs the risk of giving the right answers to questions that nobody is asking. Equally, when it comes to our evangelistic practices, the danger in 'doing what we have always done' is that many of those practices become increasingly culturally marooned, and yet, because they are so much a part of our evangelical heritage, we cease to think about them. We lose the ability to be self-critical.

Much of this book will try to give fresh perspectives on some of these questions. Our culture has clearly had a significant impact on our approaches to evangelism, and in some ways rightly so. But I hope I've made the case that cultural change should never be the driver of what we do. Nonetheless, if we treat cultural change as a mirror to all that we do, it may help us to ask the right kinds of questions in the light of scripture, and find ways to move forward.

Questions

- To what extent do you think we live in a secular society today?

- Which other words would you use to describe today's culture – and do you think Newbigin's idea of 'pagan' is helpful?

- Which of Berger's three categories do you like the best, and why?

- How might your understanding of today's culture have an impact on the way you practise evangelism in the future?

Part 1

Evangelism and the New Testament

3

What is evangelism?

Paul Weston

'Evangelism' is one of those words that tends to conjure up all the wrong kinds of mental image: the intrusive salesman, the insistent Christian, the big black Bible, the preacher's embarrassing altar calls, and so forth. If you repeat the word fast and often enough, you can even be mistaken for talking about 'vandalism' – which fits the negative stereotype beautifully and emphasises the political incorrectness of evangelism in a culturally pluralistic society. So there's some rescuing to do if we are to shed the negative cultural overtones often associated with the idea of evangelism and begin to think more positively about it. But how?

One way of doing this would be to look at the word itself. You'll find that our English word 'evangelism' is an invented word that is not found as such in the New Testament. Its earliest usage in English, according to the Oxford English Dictionary, dates back to the middle of the 17th century, when the English philosopher Francis Bacon wrote in his book *New Atlantis* that England was 'saved from infidelitie... through the Apostolicall and Miraculous Evangelisme of S. Bartholomew'. Good old St Bartholomew! The dictionary also explains that the use of the suffix '-ism' at the end of English words originated as a way of describing general 'categories' of activity, providing 'class-names' or 'systems of theory or practice'.

Some of the church's hesitations about the idea of evangelism can be traced back to this English etymology. As soon as you start categorising things, you tend by the very nature of the operation to differentiate some things from other things. You could argue that this has certainly happened in the case of evangelism. As a result, evangelism is often seen as a standalone activity which has lost its 'connectedness'. It is somehow distinct from the rest of Christian life and may suggest a kind of bolt-on module or skill that must be first acquired and then added to the normal Christian life. In line with other words that describe 'categories of activity', the word 'evangelism' has also a habit of putting its emphasis fairly and squarely upon human beings as its agents. Evangelism has come to be seen as something that *we* do. It is *our* responsibility to evangelise our friends, neighbours and colleagues. As a categorising word, then, it tends to dehumanise the idea and give the impression of systems and techniques rather than personal interaction and friendship. This impression only encourages the sense that evangelism is rather alien and threatening – certainly not something you would want to do to people you loved.

A far better way of understanding what is meant by the word 'evangelism' is to rediscover and reappropriate the biblical roots that have been somewhat masked by the English word. It is, in fact, derived from three related Greek New Testament words: *euangelisasthai*, a verb occurring 52 times in the New Testament and meaning 'to tell good news', *euangelion*, a noun used 72 times to identify the good news (or 'gospel') that is being announced, and finally the word *euangelistes*, which occurs just three times (Acts 21:8; Ephesians 4:11; 2 Timothy 4:5) and is used for the person gifted in announcing the good news.

I want, therefore, to rescue the word by refilling it with biblical meaning. In doing so, I want to show three things. First, far from being a 'depersonalised' activity, evangelism in the New Testament is understood as the instinctive sharing of good news. Second, rather than seeing evangelism as our responsibility, the New Testament writers understand our role in evangelism firmly within the flow of God's activity in bearing witness to himself. Finally, instead of seeing evangelism as a standalone activity, distinct from the rest of discipleship, the New Testament suggests that real evangelism is the natural overflow of an authentic Christian life.

Evangelism as the instinctive sharing of good news

We begin with the noun *euangelion*, which simply means 'good news', – good news about Jesus and all that he has accomplished. By the nature of all pieces of good news, the good news of Jesus is something that simply has to be told. It is contagious in character. In using this term, the early Christian writers were taking over a word used in their contemporary world that would have evoked feelings of celebration and spontaneous sharing. It was used for the celebration of the emperor's birthday, it was used by returning armies to announce that a victory had been gained, and it was used by parents who wanted to share with their friends and neighbours the joyful announcement of a new birth.

Think of any contemporary situation in which you felt that there was good news that you simply had to share with others: family achievements, sports victories or personal hopes being fulfilled. That's the feeling associated with these 'evangel' words in the New Testament. They are 'good news' events: joyful, spontaneous and people-focused.

The gospel accounts very soon convey the aura of 'good news' that focused on the activities of Jesus. All that he did and said was so deeply and profoundly attractive that 'great crowds followed him from Galilee, the Decapolis, Jerusalem, Judea, and from beyond the Jordan' (Matthew 4:25). Jesus was 'good news' in compelling and remarkable ways.

First, his actions were simply sensational. People were being healed; evil spirits were being summoned out of people; the created order was being put back into its proper shape and order. Around Jesus, the world became the very place that we instinctively feel it was meant to be – and this feeling gathered pace quickly. Mark describes the first day in Jesus' public ministry as packed with incident – healings, exorcisms and crowds. 'They were all amazed,' he reports, 'and they kept on asking one another, "What is this? A new teaching – with authority! He commands even the unclean spirits, and they obey him"' (Mark 1:27). 'At once,' Mark says, 'his fame began to spread throughout the surrounding region of Galilee' (v. 28). People simply found themselves talking about Jesus to their friends and neighbours, so that the message about him spread like wildfire. This is the first occurrence of 'evangelism' in the gospel accounts, and it happened quite spontaneously, on day one. That's what the New Testament means by 'evangelism'.

Second, Jesus' teaching was like nothing that had been heard before. He spoke with an 'authority' that was hard to define but was unmistakable. The crowds 'were astounded at his teaching', writes Mark, 'for he taught them as one having authority, and not as the scribes' (1:22). His hearers knew that through what Jesus said, they were connecting with something deeply life-giving and extraordinarily powerful. It was like hearing a live concert in all its different dimensions of sound for the first time, when all you've had before are the distorted dynamics of a scratchy 78rpm record.

Third, his actions were inclusive. They brought into the arena of God's presence and mercy people who had previously been excluded – tax collectors (who were often seen as collaborators with the occupying Romans), 'sinners' who were ritually excluded from the activities of Jewish religious life, women who were seen as second-class citizens, and even Samaritans and pagans, who were deemed to be racially inferior. All were invited by Jesus in that most powerful of actions for which he became notorious: 'table-fellowship'. To eat with Jesus was a sign of acceptance into the kingdom, of true fellowship with God. He quickly became notorious for such outrageous actions, which he himself acknowledged: 'The Son of Man came eating and drinking, and they say, "Look, a glutton and a drunkard, a friend of tax collectors and sinners!"' (Matthew 11:19). Established religious assumptions and practices were being turned upside down, the temple authorities were being outraged, but the marginalised and those beyond the religious pale were suddenly finding themselves invited to become insiders. This really was *euangelion*, 'good news'!

By relating the story of a leper, Mark personalises the spontaneity with which people simply had to talk about Jesus after coming into contact with him (Mark 1:40–45). The man comes to Jesus and says to him, 'If you choose, you can make me clean' (v. 40). Jesus is immediately 'moved with pity', stretches out his hand and says, 'Be clean!' (v. 41). The impact is instant: the leper is healed. Then, despite Jesus' stern warning that he should not tell anyone, for fear that Jesus' ministry be misunderstood and possibly derailed, the man 'went out and began to proclaim it freely, and to spread the word, so that Jesus could no longer go into a town openly, but stayed out in the country; and people came to him from every quarter' (v. 45).

Here is the essential pattern of New Testament evangelism. It was a spontaneous, irrepressible urge to tell other people about the Jesus whom you had met, who had transformed your life. People like the leper were doing it long before others sat down and invented a rather odd word for their behaviour. How we need to recover this original and spontaneous evangelistic energy in our own day! Evangelism is about *good news*.

Evangelism in the slipstream of God's own witness

As we saw at the outset, another of the tendencies of our word 'evangelism' is that it puts the emphasis in sharing the gospel upon

Christians as if they were the sole agents in the operation. This can easily produce a sense of despair and failure, encouraging the feeling that we really are on our own.

This is not the picture of evangelism that we find in the New Testament. Rather, the sharing of the good news by believers is part of God's wider evangelistic enterprise, which takes in the whole of the created order and in which God himself is the primary agent. In this context, what we do is secondary and dependent on what he is doing in and through us. We are not alone. Evangelism is slipstreaming in God's own witness to himself.

Let me explain by returning to the gospel narrative. As the story develops, we find Jesus heading for a crisis. Roughly the second half of each of the four gospels pictures the 'powers' beginning to close in on Jesus as events start to move towards his arrest, trial and crucifixion. What now? Suddenly the good news project that had seemed unstoppable appears to be coming off the rails. Each of the gospel writers pictures in different ways the sense of bewilderment, disbelief and sheer terror among the disciples at the prospect of Jesus' departure and death. Mark, for example, records the dawning of this reality three times as he starts the second half of his story (8:31; 9:31; 10:32–34). Jesus' threefold announcement of his coming suffering and death is set by Mark in a cyclical pattern in which, on each occasion, there is an immediate refusal or inability by the disciples to grasp what Jesus is saying, followed by teaching from Jesus about what it means to follow him as the crucified Messiah (8:32—9:1; 9:32–37; 10:35–45).

John records the disciples' fear and foreboding at the prospect of Jesus' death. Jesus himself refers to it when he tells them, 'Do not let your hearts be troubled' (John 14:1), repeating it in verse 27 ('Do not let your hearts be troubled, and do not let them be afraid'). An underlying sense of fear forms the backdrop to Jesus' final words to the disciples before he is arrested.

The crucifixion itself has the immediate effect of dispersing Jesus' followers in fear and panic as they try to come to terms with what has happened. Any thought of evangelism turns into shock, panic and denial. Mark records Jesus' prediction that when the shepherd is struck down, 'the sheep will be scattered' (Mark 14:27, fulfilling Zechariah 13:7), and then confirms that 'all of them deserted him and fled' (v. 50). All four gospels describe Peter denying that he ever knew Jesus (Matthew 26:69–75; Mark 14:66–72; Luke 22:54–62; John 18:25–27), and a young man (perhaps Mark himself) is pictured running away from the trial scene in just his underwear to escape the trouble (Mark 14:51–52). Then, in the following few days, the disciples are uniformly pictured in siege mentality – behind locked doors 'for fear of the Jews' (John 20:19).

Clearly the crucifixion was cataclysmic for the mindset of the disciples. Evangelism was easy when the news was so obviously good; it almost told itself. There was an impetus to it as people were naturally drawn to Jesus by all that was happening. But what next? How can you draw people to someone who's dead? What do you say?

The resurrection is clearly the answer to such a quandary, and Luke's second book, the Acts of the Apostles, describes vividly how this same group of ordinary people went on to gain a reputation among unbelievers as those who were 'turning the world upside down' (Acts 17:6). But *how* was the resurrection the catalyst to early evangelism? If we are not careful, we can go on making the early Christians the agents of evangelism because the resurrection has successfully re-energised them with a better-sounding message!

The truth of the matter is somewhat differently pictured in the New Testament and is one of the keys to a right understanding of evangelism. If we are constantly having to gear ourselves up for a bit of evangelism, we have rather missed the point. But if God is doing something and is calling us to join in with it, then a rather different picture emerges. It's the slipstreaming idea again.

We get a flavour of the early church dynamic in evangelism on the day of Pentecost, recorded in Acts 2. I'm not interested here in the extraordinary events of the day itself, but in what Peter actually says. When we read his speech, we get a strong sense both that the gospel is something that God brings about and that speaking about it is something that the Holy Spirit inspires.

Note Peter's emphasis: the good news about Jesus and all that he did is something that comes out of God's initiative. 'Jesus of Nazareth, a man attested to you by God with deeds of power, wonders, and signs that God did through him among you, as you yourselves know – this man, handed over to you according to the definite plan and foreknowledge of God, you crucified and killed by the hands of those outside the law' (Acts 2:22–23). But 'this Jesus God raised up, and of that all of us are witnesses' (v. 32), and 'God has made him both Lord and Messiah, this Jesus whom you crucified' (v. 36).

Then note how Peter says that the telling of this good news – in the native languages of Jews from all around the Mediterranean – was not prompted by any kind of human agency but by the work of the Spirit. In fact, this was just what the prophet Joel had predicted many hundreds of years earlier as a sign of the last times (Acts 2:17–21).

Evangelism and the witness of the Spirit

John has a highly significant passage on just this theme. It's found in chapter 16, where Jesus is telling the disciples about the coming of the Spirit, and includes the well-known passage about the Spirit 'convicting' the world of sin, judgement and righteousness (vv. 5–11). This is often interpreted as though the Spirit were a kind of disembodied evangelist who goes alongside us and does the job of converting people without our help. There is some truth in that idea, but the primary emphasis of the passage is slightly different. We have been looking at the dramatic change that took place in the mindset of the early disciples, which propelled them out in mission and witness.

What produced the change? It was not a new feeling that they themselves were somehow able to manufacture, but a deep work of the Spirit in bringing the fractured pieces of the Jesus story together into a coherent and dynamic whole. *And this had to happen first of all in the disciples themselves.* This is what John 16 is really about. 'It is to your advantage,' Jesus says, 'that I go away, for if I do not go away, the Advocate will not come to you; but if I go, I will send him to you' (v. 7). Note those last words – 'to you' – because they need to be carried into the next sentence too. 'And when he comes [to you], he will prove the world wrong about sin and righteousness and judgement' (v. 8).

Rather than allowing the believers to move straight into the world to evangelise others, the Spirit needs first to do the work of evangelism within them. At this point, as the death of Jesus is bearing down upon the disciples, the Spirit of Jesus comes to tell them of its real meaning. He will show them first what the real meaning of sin is.

Jesus' death does not mean that *he* is the sinful one (despite the Jewish tradition that 'anyone hung on a tree is under God's curse', Deuteronomy 21:23). Rather, 'sin' lies at the feet of those who put God's Messiah to death (see Acts 2:23, 36). The Spirit will also prove to the disciples that the 'world' is wrong about righteousness, 'because,' says Jesus, 'I am going to the Father and you will see me no longer' (John 16:10). His death and departure do not, therefore, show his lack of righteousness, but the very opposite. His going to the Father proves that he is righteousness personified. Finally, the Spirit will show them who it is who is being judged on the cross. If we had stood at the foot of the cross and been told that we were watching the final stages of a cosmic battle between good and evil, we might have been forgiven for thinking that the crucified one was suffering defeat. But actually, says the Spirit, this death was a victory, for through it the 'ruler of this world has been condemned' (v. 11).

This emphasis upon the God-origins of the gospel and the evangelising of believers by the Spirit is in harmony with the

consistent witness of the New Testamen
himself who not only inspires and brings
gospel but also bears witness to their dyna
power through the energising power of t
question of 'agency' in its proper perspecti
relax. The Spirit may sometimes provoke
there to equip us in our evangelism, even giving us words when none
may naturally be forthcoming (see Mark 13:11). Speaking of God to
others is therefore a dynamic partnership. 'The Spirit of truth who
comes from the Father,' says Jesus, 'will testify on my behalf. You
also are to testify…' (John 15:26–27).

This sense of being caught up in the slipstream of God's witness to
his own good news in the power of the Spirit is at the heart of New
Testament evangelism. The primacy of the Spirit is also underlined in
Luke's narrative in Acts by the fact that Christians always seem to be
playing 'catch up' as they seek to discern where the Spirit is at work.
Consistently, he seems to be hurdling cultural and ethnic barriers,
with the church following on some way behind.[55]

This picture is very different from the caricatures that we described
at the start of the chapter. So long as we imagine that it is we who
have to do the job in our own strength, we will consistently struggle,
but if we are hungry for the evangelising work of the Spirit within
us as well as through us, we will rediscover the heart of evangelism.
I remember attending a seminar run by a church in the United States
that had seen phenomenal growth over the previous decade. It was
entitled something like 'Motivating Christians for evangelism'. It was
packed out. As the time came for the start of the session, one of the
church leaders took the stage, announced, 'You know, it can't be
done', and walked off without further comment. There was a slightly
nervous silence. Then he returned with a smile to explain. 'Many
church leaders want to know how to motivate their congregations
for evangelism, but this is to come at the issue from the wrong angle.
What they need is not a set of techniques, nor – least of all – pressure
from the leadership. What they need is to have prayed into them a

or the lost.' Where that happens, evangelism will naturally ow. It will happen in a number of different ways, of course, as God uses individuals with their own unique gifts and graces, but it will happen.

Evangelism is the overflow of an authentic Christian life

In this final section, we look at the third way in which conceptions of evangelism can go astray. By isolating evangelism as a set of techniques or skills, we can quickly separate it from the rest of Christian life. It becomes a specialist activity, which is not for everyone because some are good at it and others are not. I want to show that this is far from the case. Indeed, the New Testament suggests that real evangelism is the natural overflow of a genuine Christian life.

It is quite difficult to put together a series of texts from the New Testament on the subject of evangelism. I know because for many years I tried to do it. I was invited to many places, either to prepare Christians to take part in missions that I had been asked to lead or to speak at one-off meetings, teaching Christians how to evangelise.

Finding such texts can be done, but I always had the sneaking sense when preparing these talks that I wasn't using the New Testament in quite the way it was intended. I wasn't going against the flow of the biblical narrative but I hadn't caught what it meant to go with it. Looking through the pages of the New Testament, we get the impression (as we have already seen) that the early Christians 'did' evangelism rather well without having to be told how to do it. We don't find seminars on personal evangelism in the Acts of the Apostles, for example. There are very few explicit exhortations to personal evangelism in the epistles, either. As Roland Allen put it with delightful understatement in his classic book *The Spontaneous Expansion of the Church*, 'What we read in the New Testament is no anxious appeal to Christians to spread the Gospel, but a note here and there which suggests how the Gospel was being spread abroad.'[56]

The main reason for this, it seems, is that New Testament evangelism is integrally connected to the whole of Christian life, not hived off as some sort of specialist activity. Consider the classic texts that are often used to exhort Christians to share their faith. For example, in 1 Peter 3:15, believers are encouraged to 'give the reason for the hope that you have… with gentleness and respect' (NIV). But the context of these words is the more general exhortation to 'set apart Christ as Lord'. In this context the believers were to be always 'prepared to give an answer to everyone who asks you'. In other words, the expectation in Peter's thought is that the opportunity to speak of Christ will follow the witness of authentic Christian lives. Christian lives will raise the questions in the minds of unbelievers to which the gospel is the answer.

Colossians 4:6 is another verse often used to encourage evangelism, and understandably so. Here, too, the sharing of the gospel is not separated from the ongoing life of the believer, but is seen as a perfectly natural outworking of it. The main body of the letter has been all about Christian lifestyle, so when Paul arrives at this section, he adds particular instructions relating to witness. 'Devote yourselves to prayer,' he says (4:2). 'At the same time pray for us as well that God will open to us a door for the word, that we may declare the mystery of Christ, for which I am in prison' (v. 3). He asks for prayer that he will be able to 'reveal' the gospel (literally, 'bring it into the open') 'clearly, as I should' (v. 4). Alongside this, he urges the believers to 'conduct yourselves wisely towards outsiders, making the most of the time' (v. 5). Our lives are to be lived, says Paul, in awareness that time is valuable and may be short.

With these elements in place, Paul concludes his exhortations on sharing the good news by saying, 'Let your speech always be gracious, seasoned with salt, so that you may know how you ought to answer everyone' (v. 6). The word 'gracious' here doesn't carry the connotation of polite 'Englishness' that we sometimes associate with it. Rather, it is a form of the word 'grace' – which, in Paul's letters, nearly always refers to the grace of God in Jesus Christ – and that is probably the sense here (meaning something like 'Let your conversation be full of the love of Jesus Christ'). It is striking, too, that when Paul finally writes about what we are actually to say, he uses the word 'answer' rather than 'tell'. Like Peter, he does not see evangelism as a distinctive activity, separated from ordinary Christian life. Rather, when the Christian life is being lived wisely and authentically, it will naturally raise the questions to which the good news of Jesus is the answer.

Back to 'evangelism'

Much of this chapter has been about getting behind the rather off-putting word 'evangelism' in order to rediscover its lively biblical roots and life-giving energy. This kind of re-education is vital to do with local believers, both through teaching and (perhaps most importantly) through prayer, because the metaphors and associations that words carry in our minds have a significant impact upon our actions and motivations. It was this need for a right mental attitude that Bryan Green (a significant evangelist in Britain from the 1930s through to the 70s) used to speak of when he referred to evangelism as not so much an 'activity' as 'an attitude of mind towards God and the world'.[57]

There are many issues I haven't touched on. Perhaps, however, it is worth pointing out a simple idea that emerges from the various New Testament passages we have been studying. These passages all involve the use of words. They may be responsive words or they may be spontaneous ones, but words are at the heart of what the New Testament understands by evangelism. This is what sets the idea of evangelism apart from wider terms like 'mission'. As John Stott puts it, 'Mission describes everything the church is sent into the world to do', while to '"evangelise" in biblical usage does not mean to win converts (as it usually does when we use the word) but simply to announce the good news, irrespective of the results'.[58] Our words of witness may be few or they may be many, but their character as true witness is not dependent upon the results they may produce. Rather, their character as witness arises out of the fact that they are spoken. In the light of all this, we are called simply to bear witness to what God has done in Jesus, and we can leave all else to the Spirit.

Questions

- How would you explain the word 'evangelism' to your church congregation?

- How do we help Christians into a deeper sense that the good news of Jesus really *is* good news?

- Where do you think the Spirit is at work in your local community? What are some of the signs?

- How do we help people to understand that this is God's work and not ours?

4

Witnessing from the inside out

Paul Weston

In this chapter and the next, I want to talk in more detail about the words we use in our evangelism. What do we actually say when we evangelise? And how do we help ourselves to develop patterns of speaking that are both faithful to the gospel and culturally relevant to those who hear us? I will assume that much may have happened beforehand. We will have been developing relationships, praying for opportunities and so forth – everything that Paul talks about in the Colossians passage we were considering at the end of the last chapter. But now we get to the point of saying something. What is it? And what do we think we are doing?

Let me begin with a proposition. In a nutshell, I believe that whereas most of us tend to be 'outside-in' evangelists, Jesus was an 'inside-out' one. Many of our evangelistic methodologies have been shaped by the generations that preceded us and tend to assume too much of our hearers. We are coming out of an era (many would say that we have already left it) in which the kind of vocabulary and ideas we used meant at least something to those we were trying to reach. Nowadays the Bible is largely a foreign book, and the language of traditional Christian belief comes across as strange and unfamiliar. Yet we often persist in our evangelistic efforts as if nothing had really changed. We go on assuming a Christian framework for the 'religious' words we use, and we take for granted that our contemporaries understand the theological 'map' that will help to make sense of them.

How, then, can we evangelise? Unfortunately, there are no easy answers or instant 'fixes' to these challenges, no handy 'how-to' kits on how to share the gospel in our contemporary post-Christian society. Nonetheless, in what follows I want to make some suggestions that may help to stimulate fresh practice and confidence. My main contention is stunningly straightforward: the time is ripe for a re-examination and reappropriation of Jesus' spoken evangelistic methodology as it is recorded in the gospels. I want to defend the notion that the idea of 'evangelism' is best understood as any process that allows Jesus to bear witness to himself in his own words. I argue that this approach has often been neglected in the past but is very appropriate in engaging a postmodern story-based culture and therefore helps particularly to meet the needs of our generation.

Evangelism modern and postmodern

If we take a look at the gospel tracts or models that have been in vogue in our evangelistic methodologies over the past several decades, we will find that the majority systematise the gospel message into a number of elements, principles or propositions. These summary statements of the good news – whether it be the 'Four Spiritual Laws', the 'Bridge to Life', 'Knowing God Personally' or 'Two Ways to Live'[59] – are designed to be easily remembered and easy to pass on to others.

I don't want in any way to dismiss these approaches, which have proved so fruitful to many in the past. I simply want to raise some points to consider in relation to evangelism and the shifting patterns of contemporary culture.

First, these models tend to presuppose a grasp of Christian vocabulary in which concepts like creation, sin, wrath, judgment, atonement, salvation and so on make some sort of sense. In addition, they assume a degree of knowledge of how these doctrinal ideas fit together and relate to one another – a kind of theological 'map'. Perhaps, in a cultural context with a residue of Christian vocabulary and understanding, such presentations were at least partially comprehensible, but my experience is that they start much too far down the line for most non-Christians. The necessary grasp of basic Christian theology and vocabulary is, as we have already said, becoming increasingly rare.

Second, I wonder whether this approach to presenting the gospel reflects biblical patterns of evangelism or not. Succinct statements of the gospel are certainly present within the New Testament. You could, for example, point to Paul's summary of the identity of Jesus as Messiah in Romans 1:1–4, his overview of Jesus' redemptive work in 1 Corinthians 15:1–9 or the so-called 'hymn to Christ' in Philippians 2:5–11. In addition, the sermons recorded by Luke in Acts have been seen to follow a pattern that incorporates consistent elements.[60] Other New Testament writers, such as John, also occasionally draw together material in summary form for the benefit of readers.[61]

However, many of these examples appear in letters addressed to those who are already believers (as the examples in Romans, 1 Corinthians and Philippians demonstrate). Their function is to teach or remind believers of the faith that they have already received so that they can remember and build upon it. Then, Luke's tendency to systematise the gospel presentations in Acts can blur the fact that both the cultural context of the audience and the questions raised by the different hearers appear to be more significant in the formulation of the sermons than is the desire to systematise the message.[62] Also, the number of summary statements in the gospels is actually very small. Where they do occur, they are mostly limited to John's gospel, and they function primarily as teaching aids, drawing together and summarising material, rather than as examples that suggest a way of communicating the gospel to non-believers.

If we understand the gospel message as a summary series of statements or propositions, evangelism can be understood as the way we work towards such presentations and defend the different parts of the structure. But what can often happen is that the good news we attempt to present comes across as a kind of alien 'package', unrelated to the context of the other person's experience of life and needing to be defended from a range of perspectives that are not necessarily beneficial to sharing the good news about Jesus.

We might start, for example, by saying (1) that God created the world, continue by showing (2) how it has turned in rebellion against him, and then explain (3) that God sent Jesus to die and (4) that we might therefore be forgiven. In doing so, we cover an awful lot of theology that will need extensive unpacking and explanation, but also, before we get past Point 1, we will probably be sidetracked into having to explain why, if God created the world, it is in the state that it is. This is something of a caricature, but you get the point. We've effectively moved away from evangelism and into 'secondary' apologetics. Then we begin to panic and wonder how on earth we are going to get the discussion back to Jesus.

'Outside-in' evangelism

The style of evangelism I've just described, with its accompanying framework of assumptions about evidence and apologetics, is what I will call an 'outside-in' approach. When a question is raised by a non-Christian, the evangelist seeks to work towards a presentation of the gospel either by means of his or her own opinions ('It's interesting you say that, but I think that...') or by means of some form of rational supporting evidence ('There is actually enough good evidence for you to take Christianity seriously...' or 'I'm sure we can agree that...'). What follows is usually a discussion about relative assumptions and presuppositions in which the evangelist's thinking is pitted more or less effectively against that of the listener. To be sure, this method often stimulates the mind but it rarely focuses upon the gospel. My own experience of this type of approach is that too much time is spent arguing around the philosophical and historical 'fringes' of the gospel, seldom reaching the point of explaining the good news itself.

'Inside-out' evangelism

My own practice of evangelism changed when I took a closer look at the gospel material. In contrast to a style of evangelism that revolved around effectively packaging the gospel in a schema that I could remember and reuse, the gospel material seemed much more fluid and – in a proper sense – 'occasional'. As Walter Hollenweger has put it, 'We find everywhere the same pattern: the starting point of Jesus' evangelism is mostly (though not always) a question, or the concrete situation of the people around him... New Testament evangelism does not start from a proposition. It starts from a situation.' He continues, 'Where we can observe the process of evangelism in the New Testament it is almost always in the form of stories which are sparked off by the situation of the listeners and worked out in dialogue with them.'[63]

This immediately set me thinking. Why is it that the gospel materials are as they are, with a whole variety of ways in which Jesus describes the meaning of the kingdom? If Jesus had been more formulaic, the gospels would have been a great deal shorter, with the content arranged differently. But, as Hollenweger puts it, 'One has to account for the fact that the four evangelists thought it vital to describe Jesus's evangelism *as a dialogical and situational approach*. There can be no doubt that they thought this approach essential to the content of the Good News.'[64]

The first thing to notice is that most of Jesus' evangelistic opportunities arose out of ordinary conversations – often about secular and seemingly mundane concerns. For example, the sublime teaching on his identity as the one through whom men and women would worship God the Father 'in Spirit and in truth' begins with a simple request to a Samaritan woman for a drink on a hot day (John 4:7–26). Again, in answer to a question about wealth and inheritance recorded in Luke 12:13, Jesus sidesteps the responsibility of arbitrating between the questioner and his brother (v. 14) and instead uses the opportunity to point up the folly of greed by telling the story of the 'rich fool' (vv. 16–21). In the light of the imminent coming of the kingdom, what's really needed, he says, is 'richness towards God' (v. 21). On another occasion, a lawyer's question, 'Who is my neighbour?' (Luke 10:29), prompts Jesus to tell the story that has come to be known as the parable of the good Samaritan. Once again, a seemingly mundane question is taken as an opportunity to show that, in the kingdom of God, accepted thinking about family and 'bonds' is reorientated to include those hitherto considered to be racially impure or inferior (vv. 29–37). The story ends in a challenge to a radical change of perspective and action: 'Go and do likewise' (v. 37).

A second thing to notice in these evangelistic encounters is that Jesus neither over-systematises the message nor appears to be working towards any kind of schematic gospel presentation. On the contrary, he responds to each question on its own terms and addresses it in the light of the coming kingdom of God. By doing so, he not only sheds light on the meaning of the gospel itself but also calls for a particular response of faith. In fact, nearly all the stories and 'sermons' we know so well from the gospels (which we often detach from their original settings) started from specific questions and issues raised by sceptics and listeners in the course of Jesus' travels. They were not 'setpiece' sermons prepared for formal religious occasions but brilliant examples of Jesus' conversational evangelism in action. No question is outside the scope of the kingdom's relevance, for the kingdom of God is about the rightful rule of God over all matters, both secular and sacred – our finances, our relationships, human identity, neighbourliness, social responsibilities, and so forth.

A third point is the number of times Jesus uses questions in the course of his evangelistic conversations. The statistics are striking: Matthew's gospel records 94 questions on the lips of Jesus, Mark records 59, Luke has 82 and John has 49. Questions come in different categories, of course. Some could be described as 'closed' questions, in the sense that they only require a one-word answer (for example, 'Are you free?'). Others are 'open', in that they invite a deeper level of sharing, either by asking for more information or by inviting some sort of emotional response (such as 'How did you feel about that?'). Most of Jesus' questions are in the second category, either inviting his hearers to reflect on what he has just said to them or challenging them to think more deeply about the words they themselves have spoken.[65]

Jesus as an example in evangelism

I want to suggest that the 'primary' evangelistic material in the New Testament is to be found in the gospel accounts themselves. This approach seems to make best sense of the gospel narratives as we have them, and indicates that an integral part of their purpose is not just to disciple believers but to 'evangelise' non-believers. They are not simply stories that help to 'illustrate' the gospel, which is to be found later in the more 'doctrinal' parts of the New Testament. No, these stories are themselves the substance of good news about Jesus.

John's gospel is the most explicit in this respect, stating that his collection of Jesus stories is written down 'so that you may come to believe that Jesus is the Messiah, the Son of God, and that through believing you may have life in his name' (John 20:31). The positioning of this climactic statement is straight after the post-resurrection story about 'doubting Thomas' (vv. 24–29). Thomas was not present when Jesus first revealed himself to the disciples after his resurrection, and when they tell him that they have seen Jesus, he says, 'Unless I see the mark of the nails in his hands, and put my finger in the mark of the nails and my hand in his side, I will not believe' (v. 25).

When Jesus appears to the disciples a week later, Thomas is with them and comes to see that Jesus is indeed 'Lord and God' (v. 28). Jesus responds with a question – 'Have you believed because you have seen me?' – and then a statement: 'Blessed are those who have not seen and yet have come to believe' (v. 29). The question brings up the potential problem for the disciples in their missionary task, that bringing people to faith must surely be related to seeing Jesus in the flesh. But the statement transcends this limitation and opens up the possibility of a saving faith that is no longer dependent upon seeing Jesus in person. In the summary verse that follows (v. 31) John says, in effect, that his intention in writing the gospel is precisely to make this new kind of 'seeing' possible for future generations. In the retelling of his gospel stories, Jesus will continue to be both seen and heard, and may be met in faith and trust, even though Jesus himself has physically departed. Not only, then, do these stories proclaim Jesus by describing what he said and did, but they also effectively 're-image' him in a way that makes him truly 'present' across the ages, enabling hearers and readers in future generations both to see Jesus and to respond to him.

How might this be done? I am not suggesting for one moment that we are able to imitate or reproduce Jesus' technique. What I am suggesting is that we train ourselves to use Jesus' own words in our evangelistic conversations, and that we pray for the divine insight and the Spirit's intuitive help to connect these words with contemporary questions. We take the gospel narratives as our material starting point and seek to find the dynamic equivalents between the issues that Jesus addressed in his day and those that our contemporary hearers face in our own time. This, it seems to me, is the essence of the evangelistic task. We want to bear witness to Jesus, the good news, by allowing him to draw attention to himself in his own words.

Let me try to illustrate this line of thinking in very practical terms. For some years now, I have attempted to engage in this 'inside-out' style of apologetics by setting myself certain aims in answering the questions that non-Christians ask. I have begun to erase the 'I think...' component of my responses, which belonged to the 'outside-in' style, and have tried to start my replies along the lines of, 'It is interesting that you say that... *Jesus* was once asked a similar question and *he* said...', or, 'That's an interesting situation you describe... *Jesus* was once involved in a similar situation and *his* response was...'.

This approach seeks to bypass the more traditional 'bridging' material and cut straight to the chase. Of course there may still be a need to engage in further apologetic argument, but the aim is to prevent these secondary debates from derailing the evangelistic thrust. My aim at these points is to lead the discussion back to the words and teaching of Jesus.

Having done so, I then find it helpful to 'press the logic' of what Jesus says towards its larger implications. Jesus does this consistently, challenging his hearers to encompass the immensity of the kingdom vision and then challenging them to place their trust in him as its proper king. We should do the same. What I have found helpful in this regard is to keep in the back of my mind the four main titles used of Jesus in the sermons recorded in the Acts of the Apostles. These are 'Lord', 'Christ', 'Saviour' and 'Judge'.[66] Each represents an ultimate truth about Jesus, of which each gospel story is an illustration. We have been used to talking of Jesus as Saviour, and many of our gospel tracts have understandably majored on this aspect of his work, but the other titles are equally prominent, with the title 'Judge' being most prominent when non-Jewish audiences are being addressed (see, for example, Acts 10:42; 17:31). So I keep these end-goals in mind as I retell the stories. Sometimes the conversation will take this direction naturally, but I find it useful nonetheless as an aide-memoire.

It may be helpful at this stage to look briefly at some examples of this approach. I will first look at two of the most common questions raised by non-believers in evangelistic conversations and then comment on some of the wider themes that emerge from the gospels.

In practice: classic questions

1 'Isn't it enough just to be good?'

The saving value of 'goodness' is a common theme in evangelistic dialogue. 'I try to help my neighbours and to do my best. No one can ask for more.' Then there is the parallel observation about sincerity, which runs along the lines of 'As long as you're sincere, I don't think it really matters what you believe.'

Using an 'outside-in' approach to this question, I would probably embark on a discussion about the relative standards of 'goodness' and how we might distinguish between them. By contrast, using an 'inside-out' approach, I will be asking myself whether Jesus was faced with a similar question and, if so, how he answered it. I suggest in this context that John 6:27–29 is a very significant passage. Jesus is followed by crowds who have seen him feed 5,000 people. When they find him, he warns them not to 'work for the food that perishes, but for the food that endures for eternal life' (v. 27). John records that they then asked him what they had to do to gain God's favour: 'What must we do to perform the works of God?' (v. 28).

Isn't this essentially the kind of question about goodness that is posed by many of our contemporaries? Note, then, how Jesus answers: 'This is the work of God, that you believe in him whom he has sent' (v. 29). This answer is startling. It effectively redirects a question about the 'works' that lead to eternal life, or about the nature of 'goodness', to a question about 'belief'. By doing so, it cuts through the secondary questions and raises an intensely Christ-centred question – which, in the end, is the really important one, and is the ultimate answer to both the nature of goodness and to gaining God's favour.

So the reply to a contemporary questioner might run along the following lines: 'It's interesting that you raise the question of good deeds. Jesus was once asked a very similar question and he said that the work of God is to believe in the one he sent. In other words, the first and most important thing we must "do" is to believe in the one whom God himself sent into the world – Jesus'. The conversation at this point will no doubt develop in one of a number of directions, but my experience is that it almost always raises the question of Jesus' identity. What Jesus does constantly is to refocus the attention upon himself rather than upon other less important concerns.[67]

2 'Surely you cannot be saying that Jesus is the only way to God?'

The question about the uniqueness of Jesus will continue to be a central and provocative concern. To most people, it seems extraordinary and unacceptable that Jesus should be the *only* way by which we can be saved. Increasingly we will hear a response like, 'I think, in the end, that all religions lead to God.'

How do we answer this? Using an 'outside-in' approach, my tendency was to use the phrase 'I think' – either to fudge the issue by saying that God will, in the end, do the just thing, or try to develop arguments that justify God's fairness in the Old Testament. Either way, I found that hearers responded to my arguments about the defensibility of God's actions rather than to the gospel itself. By contrast, an 'inside-out' approach would try once more to reply along the lines of 'It's interesting you should raise that question. Jesus himself said…'. But where would we look? The most obvious place would be John 14:6–7. Here Jesus says, 'I am the way, and the truth, and the life. No one comes to the Father except through me. If you know me, you will know my Father also. From now on you do know him and have seen him.'

The most well-known part of this saying is the first clause, but for our purposes the more significant are the clauses that follow. Many postmoderns welcome the inclusiveness of Jesus but baulk at his exclusiveness. In our text the inclusivity of clause 1 is followed by the exclusivity of clause 2, which in turn is explained by Jesus' reference to his identity in clause 3. As before, our approach would seek to state Jesus' words explicitly as the response to the question raised by our listener. How the conversation proceeds will again vary, but, as in the first example, the focus of the conversation invariably comes to revolve around the identity of Jesus himself. The charge of arrogance levelled against the Christian position is not now aimed at the cleverness or content of my own arguments but is directed at the seemingly unacceptable nature of the claims of Jesus himself.

The other side to the question about Jesus' exclusiveness is, of course, what will happen to those who have never heard about him. Once again, my earlier approach was to argue for the justice of God in quite abstract and complex terms. Latterly, however, I have used Jesus' words in Matthew 11:21: 'Woe to you, Chorazin! Woe to you, Bethsaida! For if the deeds of power done in you had been done in Tyre and Sidon, they would have repented long ago in sackcloth and ashes.' At first sight this seems a strange saying to quote (especially to non-Christians), but its point is rather clear. Jesus is saying, in response to the unbelief he encounters in Galilee, that if similar things had been done in the cities of Tyre and Sidon, their inhabitants would have believed. In other words, Jesus knows the response they would have given to him, even though he has not been there. The thrust of such words is the same as the more abstract argument about God's justice, except that it is much more succinct and focuses the hearer's attention back on to Jesus and his words.

In practice: contemporary themes

If the 'inside-out' approach can be applied to common questions and objections, it can also be used to address more general themes and issues. The key, as before, is to say something from the lips of Jesus about the kingdom in the context of the seemingly mundane and worldly. We have seen that this has two aspects: to make connections between the themes that arise at work or in home life and the issues that Jesus addresses, and to use Jesus' words to address them once again. Our evangelism training courses would be considerably enhanced (and far more productive) if we were to take the issues that have arisen in our own lives and those of our friends or colleagues and ask how Jesus addressed them.

Some of our answers to these questions will surprise even ourselves. Is it possible to retell the stories of Jesus to our friends? Yes, of course. At a pub meeting on a mission, I was surprised when I heard myself relaying the story of the 'rich fool' in Luke 12 to a businessman with whom I had struck up a conversation about salaries. But why not? Isn't this precisely what evangelism is going to look like in a Christless society? If we take every opportunity to retell the gospel stories, and take the time to do so without apology, I fancy that we will be doing precisely what the earliest evangelists did, for the gospels were and are fundamentally evangelistic tools (see Mark 1:1; John 20:31).

The best way to develop these skills is in company with other Christians, taking perhaps a single issue each week and asking what Jesus said about it – whether it be on the subject of money and wealth,[68] the vanity of pride[69] or the origins and power of evil.[70] Work with these texts and try to tease out their relevance and application. You will find it a liberating discipline that will stretch and excite your thinking about evangelism, as well as challenging the way you do it.

Concluding thoughts

'Pre-' and 'proper' evangelism

In the light of what we have been saying, distinctions sometimes made between the concepts of 'pre-evangelism' and evangelism 'proper' appear to evaporate. If our aim is to work from 'inside' the gospel, there is no such thing as 'pre'-evangelism. Take Mark's gospel, for example, where the story of Jesus' ministry begins with the shortest sermon on record: 'The Kingdom of God is at hand: repent, and believe in the good news' (1:15). There is certainly nothing 'pre' about this statement. In one sense it sums up everything there is to say about the kingdom. Everything else is an implication (or 'fallout') arising from this initial stupendous statement, and it will involve a radical reorientation of both thought and action.[71] Jesus *starts*, then, with a gospel announcement and works through its implications in all that follows. It is interesting that our contemporary strategies have tended to reverse this process, starting with various 'bridging' or preparatory strategies that are designed to lead *towards* such an announcement. I will say more about this in chapter 5.

Narrative and truth

I mentioned earlier that the 'inside-out' approach may help to meet the need for relational and conversational apologetics in our contemporary postmodern setting. There are three aspects to this.

First, at a practical level, it enables a quicker engagement with the words and claims of Jesus than does a more reasoned, linear approach to apologetics. Second, at a communicational level, stories and 'narratives', rather than abstract propositions and statements, are more ideally suited to the postmodern mindset that we encounter today. People love to be told stories. They engage us and draw us in. In fact, they are fundamental to our sense of identity because they give coherence and meaning to our lives. As Alasdair MacIntyre puts it, 'We all live out narratives in our lives and... we understand our own lives in terms of narratives that we live out.'[72] An apologetic strategy that interconnects the daily narratives of our lives with the narrative of God's life – expressed in word and deed in the incarnation of Jesus – is always a good way in, but is ideally suited to a postmodern context.[73] Third, an 'inside-out' approach reveals the truth about Jesus from within the Christian narrative rather than claiming a prior philosophical truthfulness for that narrative from 'outside'. In other words, the claim that Jesus' words are true is one that authenticates itself in the process of explanation and investigation rather than having to be proved by means of arguments about the reliability of the Bible, or whatever.

Knowing the gospels

Working at this style of evangelism is exhilarating but it is also demanding. It requires us to be much more familiar with the gospel stories than is commonly the case among Christians today. The philosopher Michael Polanyi used the term 'indwelling' to describe the type of knowledge we are aiming for. He used it to refer to that intimate kind of knowledge – like knowing how to ride a bike – that becomes second nature through the process of being learnt. By 'indwelling' the skill of cycling, we are able to concentrate on further tasks (like avoiding other traffic or simply taking in the view), but we can only do these things because we already know how to cycle. In the same way, the aim in this style of evangelism is to 'indwell' the gospel material so that it becomes part of our vocabulary – available to us when we need it. When this is the case, we can then concentrate on making connections with the people to whom we are speaking. In every experience of evangelism training along these lines, I have found that this is the single biggest issue. We simply don't know the gospels well enough.

Although our contemporary setting poses great challenges to the Christian communicator, it is worth underlining the fact that postmodernity has not taken God by surprise! The rediscovery of the gospel narratives and their deployment in the work of evangelism seems to me to be one of the unused treasures of the Bible, especially appropriate in our day. May God grant us help in using them as they were originally used – for the sake of the kingdom. As John puts it, 'Jesus did many other signs in the presence of his disciples, which are not written in this book. But these are written so that you may come to believe that Jesus is the Messiah, the Son of God, and that through believing you may have life in his name' (John 20:30–31).

Questions

- What is the difference between an inside-out and an outside-in approach to evangelism?

- How might this help us to think about evangelism in our churches?

- How does the example of Jesus in the gospel stories help us to think more creatively about evangelism?

- What kinds of teaching and training would help people to use this approach in evangelism?

5

Apologetic evangelism?

Paul Weston

What is the relationship between 'evangelism' and 'apologetics'? Are they two separate things and, if so, how do we understand the role of apologetics in our contemporary context? If not, what is the relationship between them?

Like the concept of evangelism, which we looked at in chapter 3, we find that the English word 'apologetics' is not, strictly speaking, a biblical word. Furthermore, its English form doesn't help us to understand its original meaning, even suggesting that it has something to do with making an 'apology'. It derives from the Greek word *apologia*, which was used in the classical Greek legal system to describe the formal verbal defence made by the accused in response to the charges set forward by the prosecution. This legal connection can be seen in the way in which the word is sometimes used in the New Testament. Luke, for example, uses it to describe the 'defence' (*apologia*) that Paul makes before his Jewish captors in Acts 22:1, when he is arrested in Jerusalem (see also Acts 25:16). Paul himself uses it in a related way to describe the 'defence' he makes of his ministry in the face of his critics in Corinth (1 Corinthians 9:3; see 2 Corinthians 7:11 for a similar use).

This background helps to explain how the word *apologia* came to be used in a more general sense to refer to the ways in which Christians defended their faith in the face of opposition. One example is 1 Peter 3:15, where Peter urges his readers, 'Always be ready to make your defence (Gk. *apologia*) to anyone who demands from you an account of the hope that is in you' (see also Philippians 1:7, 16).

Alongside this defensive sense, however, the developing idea of apologetics also took on a more proactive dimension. This takes in Paul's thought in 2 Corinthians 10 about the 'weapons of our warfare', which 'have divine power to destroy strongholds' (v. 4). He goes on, 'We destroy arguments and every proud obstacle raised up against the knowledge of God, and we take every thought captive to obey Christ' (vv. 4–5). Here, the sense is of military engagement with other systems of belief that stand against and contradict the good news of Jesus.

There is therefore both a reactive and proactive dimension to the practice of apologetics in the New Testament. It is both a defence against attack and an attack against defences. Both these dimensions have retained their usage as the discipline of apologetics has developed over the centuries.

Apologetics and evangelism

In the previous chapter, we discussed specific responses to some contemporary questions, but in this chapter I want to explore the broader relationship of apologetics to evangelism. Is it a separate activity, perhaps preceding evangelism, as if the apologetic enterprise is like employing artillery guns to knock down the defences before sending in the evangelistic infantry? Or is it part and parcel of the same thing? My aim is to raise questions that may help us to think more biblically about this relationship.

There has been a tendency to distinguish the two activities in popular thinking. In particular, the way in which apologetics has developed in a culture influenced by the Enlightenment – with its emphasis upon reason – has tended to make the practice of apologetics a rather specialised area. Concentrating on objective arguments about proof, demonstration and evidence, it is felt to be beyond the reach of ordinary Christians. It sounds too academic, needing too much expertise, and is therefore too threatening for many of us. All this has tended to separate the practice of apologetics from the mainstream practice of Christian witness. By contrast, a number of approaches to contemporary evangelism have gone the other way, emphasising the more subjective sharing of stories and the giving of personal testimony, rather than engaging in more intellectual forms of apologetics. Although neither approach is wrong in its proper context, these distinctions have tended to drive a wedge between the practices of apologetics and evangelism.

As in the other chapters in this section of the book, I want to take a fresh look at the New Testament. In particular, I want to look at Paul's speech to the Areopagus in Athens, recorded in Acts 17, as a test case with which to explore these relationships and apply some of the findings to contemporary practice.

Paul and the Areopagus speech

There has been a lot of debate about Paul's apologetic approach at Athens, much of which tends to highlight the distinctions we have just identified. It is often said, for example, that Paul takes a different line at Athens than Peter does at Jerusalem on the Day of Pentecost in Acts 2. On the surface, of course, this is self-evident. In Acts 2, the emphasis is clearly upon argument from scripture, with Peter's approach assuming a working knowledge of the Old Testament. Such knowledge would not have existed among the non-Jewish audience that Paul was addressing at Athens.[74] In Acts 17, it is argued, Paul takes a rather different tack from Peter, arguing from what his listeners do know (their altars and poets) to what they do not know (the identity of the true God and the meaning of the resurrection of Jesus). Paul is therefore using a different tactic from

Peter's, working towards the gospel (and, by implication, scripture), rather than from it.

If this is true, we could say that what Paul does at Athens is more 'apologetic' than 'evangelistic'. This (so the argument goes) is Paul's characteristic practice elsewhere, because he is frequently described by Luke as 'arguing/dialoguing' rather than 'preaching/evangelising'. So, here in Athens, Luke refers to the fact that Paul 'argued in the synagogue with the Jews and the devout persons, and also in the marketplace every day with those who happened to be there' (Acts 17:17).

This suggestion that there is a distinction between the apologetic and evangelistic dimensions of Paul's strategy has some significant implications for our practices today. It is said that, because we live in a biblically illiterate culture, we, like Paul, need to start in 'apologetic' territory, and then move on to the more 'evangelistic' content of our message.

However, we need to face some problems with the assumption that this is what Paul was doing. To begin with, it is very clear that Luke himself thought Paul was not only 'doing apologetics' at Athens but was also 'evangelising' the Athenians, and as part and parcel of the same activity. For example, having told us that Paul 'argued' with his hearers in the synagogue and marketplace, he tells us in the very next verse that, as part of this process of argument and dialogue, Paul was 'telling the good news about Jesus and the resurrection' (literally, 'evangelising', v. 18). This immediately suggests that Luke himself saw the two activities of 'argument' and 'evangelism' as intrinsically interconnected rather than separate. In fact, when we follow up the other Lukan references to Paul's practice of 'dialoguing' and 'arguing' in Acts, it becomes clear that the starting point and content of his argument was scripture itself rather than some form of abstract argument. This implies once more that there was an intrinsic connection in the mind of Luke (and Paul) between 'argument' and 'evangelism', rather than a separation (see, for example, Acts 17:2; 19:8).

In addition, it is clear from the results of the speech that some 'became believers' (17:34), and the fact that Luke names them ('Dionysius the Areopagite and a woman named Damaris, and others with them') shows not only that they probably became founding members of the Athenian church but also that Luke really thought that Paul's speech (however skilful as a piece of apologetics) had preached the gospel on Mars Hill that day.

So, let's look more closely at Acts 17.

Paul's audience at Athens

Paul arrived in Athens ahead of his missionary companions, Silas and Timothy, who had stayed on in Berea (much further north) when Paul was whisked away following the disturbances caused by his preaching there (Acts 17:13–15). He had time on his hands and spent it wandering around the city and its marketplace, listening and looking. Luke tells us that 'while Paul was waiting for them at Athens, his spirit was provoked within him as he saw that the city was full of idols' (v. 16, RSV). The word 'provoked' is a strong one (from which we get the word 'paroxysm'), indicating a strong internal reaction – even revulsion – to what he saw as idolatry among the Athenians. Paul's response was characteristic: he started to 'argue' in the synagogue with the Jews and God-fearing Greeks, and in the marketplace with anyone who happened to be there.

In particular, Luke says that Paul spoke to a number of Epicurean and Stoic philosophers (v. 18). Their initial impressions of him were clearly mixed. Some thought he was a 'babbler' (the kind of person who picked up strange and random ideas and ran with them), while others thought he was a 'proclaimer of foreign divinities' because he kept speaking about 'Jesus and the resurrection'. So they summoned him to a meeting of the Areopagus on Mars Hill and asked him to explain his new ideas in more detail.

The Stoics and the Epicureans represented two quite different and contradictory Greek schools of thought, which disagreed at key points. On the one hand, the Stoics were pantheists. They believed that god was totally contained within the created order, and that nothing of him existed separately from it or beyond it. The Epicureans, on the other hand, believed that god was totally absent from his created order. He was not only separated from it as an independent being but had no interest in it, and, as a result, had left all things to chance. Not surprisingly, the Epicureans believed that god was essentially unapproachable and certainly incapable of being known by human beings, however 'religious' their practices were.

With even this brief insight into the contradictory nature of Paul's audience, it becomes apparent how skilful he was as an apologist. Of course, the speech was likely to have been much longer than the version Luke records, but the main features of its content are clear. Its basic theme is the true nature of God and his relationship to his creation, and Paul takes on both groups of thinkers in relevant and pointed ways.

Paul's speech

Paul begins by addressing the worldview of the Stoics. In answer to their belief that god is contained within the created order, Paul's basic point – made from a number of different angles – is that he is actually far *beyond* us (vv. 24–26). Far from being contained within the created order, he actually created the world, as 'Lord of heaven and earth', and therefore cannot possibly be thought of as living 'in shrines made by humans beings'. Moreover, he is well able to look after himself and does not need to be 'served by human hands'. Again, as Lord of the universe, he himself is the one who gives to his creatures life and breath and everything they need. Indeed, he is the one who not only determines the length of human lives but even decides the places where those lives are lived.

Next, Paul turns to the Epicureans. In answer to their belief that the supreme being is totally separate and uninterested in his world, Paul argues that he is intimately involved in it, and especially with human beings as his special creation. He is a God of grace and mercy, giving to us human beings all things so that we might seek after him and find him, for he is 'not far from each one of us' (v. 27). So intimately is he involved with his created order that it can be said that 'in him we live and move and have our being' and that we are his 'offspring' (v. 28) – as some even of their own poets had put it.

Paul then presses towards his conclusion. Here he addresses both groups by returning to the theme of idolatry, which had sparked the speech in the first place. Whatever they thought of God, the one thing they must not do is think of him as some kind of idol, made by human hands (v. 29). God is a personal being; he is the ultimate authority in the universe and will one day call all people to account. 'He will have the world judged in righteousness by a man whom he has appointed,' and has given evidence of this by raising Jesus from the dead (v. 31). Luke records that the results of Paul's speech were varied. Some scoffed at what they had heard. Others were given plenty to think about and wanted to hear more (v. 32). Still others, as we have seen, became followers of Jesus (v. 34).

A number of things stand out from Paul's approach at Athens, which are significant as we think about the skills needed in contemporary apologetics. We will come to some of these shortly. To begin with, however, it is worth noting that Paul's approach to proclaiming the gospel is one in which apologetics and evangelism are woven together. It seems futile, therefore, to make the kinds of distinction that we discussed earlier, or to try to work out which bits of the speech are 'apologetics' and which are 'evangelistic'. As Luke pictures it, the two are interwoven.

Reconnecting apologetics and evangelism

In chapter 2 we looked at some of the cultural influences on contemporary approaches to evangelism. The influence of the Enlightenment on our practices has been both far-reaching and profound. Here I want to develop that idea further by suggesting that part of this influence has been to fuel the separation of apologetics and evangelism, with the former tending to become over-rationalised and the latter over-sentimentalised.

To trace the history of apologetics in the culture of the west is well beyond the scope of this short chapter, but we can at least point out some of its relevant features. First, a number of apologetic strategies in the west have taken a rationalistic direction, directly in response to the dominant intellectual atmosphere associated with the culture of the Enlightenment. In this context, it was felt that the good news of the gospel needed to be shown to be 'reasonable', that there was 'good evidence' to back it up and that God's existence could even be 'proved'. This general strategy helps to explain, in part, the rise and prominence of 'evidentialist' styles of apologetics over the past couple of centuries: for example, philosophical arguments about the existence of God, historical evidence for the existence of Jesus, the defence of the reliability of the New Testament documents and – perhaps supremely – evidences for the resurrection. These were sometimes considered to be necessary ground-clearers before effective evangelism could take place.

However, this evidentialist strategy has left some apologists stranded in the wake of significant cultural changes. With the onset of postmodernity, much of the dominant objective rationalism of the Enlightenment has been either questioned or dethroned, and perceptions about the nature of truth and how it is recognised are quickly moving in new directions.

As a result of all this, some forms of evidential apologetics appear no longer to have the same 'cash value' as they once did. Arguments for the historical reliability of the resurrection, for example, often fall on deaf ears. Whereas, in previous generations, the acceptance of the historical basis of the resurrection was assumed to be the point at which a sceptic simply had to capitulate and become a Christian, now the sceptic is more likely to respond, 'So what?' My own experience as a university evangelist 30 years ago was that most people at the time were much more upfront about the need to be persuaded of the possibility of the supernatural than they are now. Nowadays, those brought up on *The X-Files*, *Heroes* or *Twilight* have less of a problem with the spiritual world. Their dominant questions are not so much about the supernatural but about whether Christianity can claim that it is the only way to find God.

I found myself, as an evangelist, beginning to ask new questions about what I was doing in this strange new world. It took me back to the New Testament with a fresh pair of eyes and a new set of questions. Was it the case, for example, that the classic evidentialist defence of the reliability of the resurrection – with its appeal to 'reason' and 'evidence' – formed a necessary evangelical defence of the gospel or simply a culturally appropriate one? And, more fundamentally, did the New Testament writers try to convince their readers in this kind of way, or were they more concerned to persuade on other grounds?

One of my conclusions at the time was the sobering realisation that much of my own apologetic strategy had been subconsciously based on the assumption that the gospel could be viewed and weighed up from a neutral vantage point. My role as an apologist was to persuade my hearers (who stood where I stood and could therefore be persuaded by arguments from reason and evidence) that the gospel was true. In the patterns of apologetic that have developed from this belief, Christian apologists see both themselves and their non-Christian hearers as standing outside the sphere of the gospel, and understand their job as one of rational persuasion: 'Can't you see with me that the gospel makes sense?' Once this 'reasonableness' is considered to be the key component in the weighing up of the gospel's claims, then evidentialist arguments for the reliability of the resurrection accounts, or the historical existence of the man named Jesus, or the reliability of the New Testament more generally, become key components in our apologetic strategy.

But such a vantage point doesn't exist. As John Reader puts it, 'There is no "view from nowhere", only a variety of views from somewhere.'[75] At this point in my thinking, two particular questions began to stand out. The first was to ask the basic question: on what grounds am I trying to commend the gospel of Jesus Christ, and how far do I believe they will get me? My own experience over the years has been that while I may get some way towards producing theists and deists by the arguments of reason, I will never get very far in the business of producing Christians. The reason for this is actually very straightforward. The heart of the Christian faith is essentially rather *un*reasonable. The idea that God should come into the world in the form of Jesus Christ and die on a cross for the sake of fallen humanity remains, for most postmoderns (and moderns, for that matter), either a 'stumbling block' or simply 'foolishness' – just as it was for first-century Jews and Greeks.[76] (This is not to say, of course, that the gospel is ultimately unreasonable. But it is to say that it is properly reasonable only within its own biblical framework, and that this reasonableness is comprehended only by a mind that has been divinely enlightened and converted by the gospel itself.)

As a result, my second question was: what might strategies of evangelism and apologetics look like if they begin from a gospel starting point rather than some supposedly 'external' and 'neutral' one? As I developed this thought, I became increasingly convinced that this is the major style of apologetic found within the New Testament, and that apologetics therefore has to be done from within the scriptural framework of the gospel itself. Although many of our evangelistic enquirers' courses start with 'evidence' as the rational way into exploring the Christian faith, the New Testament writers are more direct. 'The beginning of the good news of Jesus Christ, the Son of God,' says Mark in his opening sentence; 'In the beginning was the Word, and the Word was with God, and the Word was God,' says John 1:1.

We looked in chapter 2 at John's portrayal of the resurrection and saw there that Thomas' concerns about evidence ('Unless I see...'), were answered by John's insistence that it is through the retelling of the stories of Jesus recorded in the gospel that future generations will 'see' Jesus and be blessed in doing so. Again, if we ask at what level Luke's portrayal of the resurrection functions apologetically, we have to conclude that it presupposes just this sort of 'revelational' understanding of God's actions within history – as spoken either by the scriptures or by Jesus himself – as the basis for a right understanding of the resurrection itself (Luke 24:5–7, 25–27, 32, 44–49). The disciples (and the subsequent readers of the gospel) are told that they will only have access to the truth about the resurrection once they have begun to understand the nature and content of this revelation.

This brings us back to Paul at Athens. As we noted earlier, there are clear differences in specific content between Paul's words here and those of Peter at Pentecost, with Paul understandably not quoting directly from the Old Testament as Peter did in Jerusalem. However, just like Peter at Pentecost, Paul is interpreting what he sees in front of him *in the light of the biblical narrative*. He is reinterpreting the Epicurean and Stoic conceptions of God's character in the light of God's revelation of himself in scripture. This appears different on the surface only because the audiences are so different; his strategy is precisely the same as Peter's – to read his hearers' worldview through the lens of scripture.

What skills do we need to cultivate in our own day? In the light of the discussion in this chapter, as well as the previous one, I think it is more helpful to think of evangelism as an 'art' than as a 'science', being in the proper sense adaptive rather than programmatic. By that I mean that what we say (if it is not to bypass our listeners entirely) must connect both with real lives and with the questions they feel, but it must then offer the transformation that the gospel of Jesus embodies. This is what Jesus did, paying serious attention to the concrete questions and circumstances that he encountered and then re-hanging those questions in the light of the coming kingdom. It is also what Peter and Paul did, in parallel ways, in their speeches in Acts. To different audiences they took the questions presented and re-hung them in the light of the great biblical narrative. What skills will this involve?

Cultivating the art of listening

First, we need to cultivate the art of stepping back from our surroundings, to listen to our culture as though (like Paul in Athens) we were visiting it for the first time. Paul had clearly attuned himself to the multiple dimensions of the Athenian culture that he was visiting. As we have seen, he had reached the heart of the Stoic and Epicurean conceptions about 'god' and had understood their ways of thinking in the wider cultural context of a more general search for the divine. As a result, this became Paul's starting point as he addressed the gathering of the Areopagus, and the concept of misplaced 'worship' provided him with the bridging idea to the gospel itself. 'Athenians, I see how extremely religious you are in every way. For as I went through the city and looked carefully at the objects of your worship, I found among them an altar with the inscription, "To an unknown god." What therefore you worship as unknown, this I proclaim to you' (vv. 22–23).

We too need to be good listeners, hearing and respecting before speaking. So listen to other people's stories; try to pick up and identify their emphases and themes, the hopes and fears that they talk about. Pay attention to the wider 'texts' presented by songs and media stories, and try to identify once more the hopes and fears that they speak of. In a similar way to Paul at Athens, we need to develop the skills of being cultural listeners. In a previous chapter, we examined briefly the so-called secular context in which we now live in the west. We saw that the setting of faith over against secularity is an unhelpful way of understanding what is going on around us, but we saw also how the exercise of worship continues to characterise human behaviour. Like Paul at Athens, this is a very good place to start. A good question, therefore, to ask of the communities we inhabit is this: how and what does it worship? Like Paul, we need to be 'worship spotters'.

Cultivating the art of discerning

Having listened to (and watched) those around us, part of the art of evangelism and apologetics is to discern the meaning of what we hear in the light of the gospel of Jesus. This is what Paul does so effectively during his time in Athens. He listens and then discerns the meaning of what he hears through the lens of the gospel of Jesus. He does it so well that, by the time he comes to speak, he has already thought through answers to questions like 'How is the worship of this community affirmed by the gospel? How is that worship to be redirected? Where are the connecting points between its hopes and fears and the story of Jesus? Where are the points of disjunction?'

Paul's approach at Athens can profitably be compared with his strategy elsewhere – for example, at Pisidian Antioch in Acts 13 or at Lystra in Acts 14 – as well as with the other apostolic sermons recorded in Acts (notably by Peter at Pentecost in Acts 2, or in Jerusalem in Acts 3). Two things stand out.

The first is that there are different but connected ways in which to share the good news, each of which depends upon the hearers. Paul is therefore not constrained by any single way of communicating the gospel of Jesus. In his Athens speech, for example, he omits any reference to the death of Jesus – but, as we have seen, there is no suggestion in Luke's narrative that Paul therefore wasn't preaching the gospel. Rather, Paul concentrates on the resurrection, partly because he was asked to do so (see 17:18–19) but also because the resurrection (and coming judgement) directly challenged his listeners' worldview.

Developing skill in discernment is increasingly important in our contemporary culture, which is becoming less and less familiar with the biblical narrative. Our ways of presenting the good news of Jesus will all find their focus in the central events of Jesus' life, death and resurrection, but will often start at different points, take varying routes, concentrate upon different aspects of the gospel and come at the underlying issues from distinctive angles, depending upon our prior 'listening'.

At heart, this is an exercise in imagination, or *re*imagination. Walter Brueggemann has done much to help us understand the biblical storyline as an invitation to reimagine contemporary life in an alternative frame of reference. He argues that the biblical stories are essentially designed 'to generate alternative futures'[77] and that the aim of evangelism is a '*transformed consciousness* that results in an altered perception of world, neighbour, and self, and an authorisation to live differently in that world'.[78] The evangelist's task is one of invitation – as Trevor Hart puts it – 'to step into the [biblical] narrative and consider the world from within it, to see whether it does not make more sense than other alternative stories told about it. This is... essentially an appeal to the imagination, an invitation to construe the world differently, to entertain the possibility that things are other than we have hitherto supposed.'[79] I like the comment of Alasdair MacIntyre, talking of a particular approach to apologetics as 'Tell me your story and I will show you that it only becomes intelligible within this framework'.[80] He could have been talking about Paul at Athens.

Cultivating the art of speaking

Do our words address people where they are? It is a sad characteristic of much of our evangelism that they don't! Is this because we have tended to speak before we've spent enough time listening? Paul's message at Athens clearly did communicate, for precisely the reasons we have explored. His was, of course, a more public speech than most of the conversations that we will have, but the same principles apply. He started where people were – in this case, with the inscription 'To an unknown god' that he had seen on an altar in the city. He kept in touch with his audience throughout his speech, both with their material world (what they were reading and seeing) and with their perceptual one (what they were thinking). And he brought them face-to-face with the heart of the good news: Jesus Christ, risen and exalted, before whom every knee must bow.

Questions

- How would you describe the relationship between apologetics and evangelism?

- What experiences did Paul have to process to give the speech that Luke records in Acts 17?

- How might this chapter help people who feel they don't have answers to give?

- How do we encourage each other to listen together more attentively to what's going on around us?

6

Evangelism in three 'spaces'

Paul Weston

In working with young people in America, do not try to call them back to where they were, and do not try to call them to where you are, as beautiful as that place might seem to you. You must have the courage to go with them to a place that neither you nor they have ever been before.[81]

I suspect that the dominant motif behind much of our thinking about evangelism in the west is still that of 'come and see'. The church has good news to share, which the world desperately needs to hear. But the movement we imagine taking place in this process is often one that involves others coming over to where we are, to join our group, our congregation, our church. If we have programmes and strategies for evangelism in our churches, they are often characterised by this 'come to us' mentality.

We will call this 'first-space' evangelism.

There is a great deal of truth here, of course. After all, Jesus himself said that it would be the life and vibrancy of Christian communities that would make a vital and attractive appeal to those who are currently outside the faith,[82] so it's not surprising that 'first-space' evangelism is a central feature of New Testament mission. But (perhaps especially in the west) this kind of approach can subtly grow to dominate our thinking, making us imagine that this is the only model of evangelism and mission. In the New Testament, it sits in harness with another model, which is about the movement away from the church in order to 'go and tell'.

We will call this 'second-space' evangelism.

I want to suggest in this chapter that the primary model of evangelism in the New Testament is neither of these things, though it does involve both. Actually, it is more profound than either of them, if they are considered on their own. It is part of a deeper process in which both teller and receiver, sender and sent, may grow into new possibilities. It's about a 'third space'.

Church as 'first space'

A recurring theme of this book has been that our culture is shifting fast. Partly as a result of this, we have seen that the church – having grown used to a position of some significance – is losing ground very rapidly. In my own denomination, there have been a number of initiatives to try to address this challenge. In 1988, for example, the Lambeth Conference of Anglican Bishops was significant in trying to refocus priorities and set new patterns of thinking in relation to evangelism and mission. Its report (entitled *The Truth Shall Make You Free*) stated:

> Our Churches are always in danger of diverting the energies and focus of their members from their essential task of mission, to an introverted preoccupation with ecclesiastical concerns. We call our Churches and all Christians back to mission and we urge them to respond with all their heart to our Lord's commission to go out into the world in his name.[83]

One of its central challenges was the need to move away from what it called 'maintenance' models to 'mission' models of ministry. 'The pressing needs of today's world,' it said, 'demand that there be a massive shift to a "mission" orientation throughout the Communion... At the heart of this would be a revolution in the attitude to the role of the laity. Such a revolution would enable us to see every Christian as an agent of mission.'[84]

Nearly 25 years on, it is still a matter of debate to what extent this vision has been implemented. The widely embraced 'Decade of Evangelism' in the 1990s certainly helped to refocus the energy of congregations on outreach, but the majority of these initiatives – effective though they may have been in the short term – did not greatly affect the underlying assumptions of either church leaders or congregations. They represented a concentrated effort at outreach, from which most were happy (and somewhat relieved) to settle back into a more comfortable 'maintenance' mode. If outreach is on the agenda at all in our churches, it is easy to see how the 'first-space' model, with its 'come and see' strategy, has dominated.

Church and 'second-space' evangelism

Within its longer-term history, however, the church in the west has managed to develop 'second-space' strategies. Indeed, the modern 'missionary movement', which began as far back as the late 15th century and reached its heyday in the 18th and 19th centuries, was essentially built around a 'go and tell' strategy. Its impact on the shape of the modern world, for both good and ill, has been nothing short of extraordinary.

Yet this missionary impetus was often marked by a paradox, for, despite being 'second space' in its energy, it often resulted in the establishment of lots more 'first spaces': the only difference was that they were now abroad. The reason was that, particularly in the early periods of colonial expansion, the outgoing missionaries felt that a central part of their role was to introduce 'civilisation' to the 'natives' as part of a process of 'Christianisation'. There was very little desire – or even perceived need – to work at the task of what we would now call contextualisation. As the great South African missionary analyst David Bosch put it, 'By the time the large-scale western colonial expansion began, western Christians were unconscious of the fact that their theology was culturally conditioned; they simply assumed that it was supracultural and universally valid. And since western culture was implicitly regarded as Christian, it was equally self-evident that this culture had to be exported together with the Christian faith.'[85]

As a result of this type of assumption, the mission station often became the typical result of missionary activity on foreign soil – centring around a church building, a school and maybe a hospital. It was from this 'home base' that evangelistic and missionary initiatives were carried out, and it was back to this home base that the missionaries' efforts were directed. Not surprisingly, the resulting shape of Christianity experienced by the local population was foreign and alien, influenced more by the sending culture than by any real attempt on the part of the missionaries to understand their audiences and contextualise the gospel.

The resulting mindset created its own agenda, of course, both at home and overseas, setting expectations and establishing persistent assumptions about church, mission and, more fundamentally, even the gospel itself. In the light of over 20 years' missionary experience in India, Lesslie Newbigin could still write in the 1960s that the church's 'typical shape in the eyes of its own members as well as those outside has been not a band of pilgrims who have heard the word "Go", but a large and solid building, which, at its best, can only say "Come", and at its worst says, all too clearly, "Stay away".'[86] This 'first-space' mentality continues to dominate our thinking, it seems.

Revisiting the New Testament

There are a number of ways in which a fresh reading of the New Testament challenges these inherited assumptions about church and mission.

To begin with, a 'first-space' mentality (or the concept of maintenance) would have meant very little, if anything, to James, Peter or Paul. The fledgling church was still in an embryonic state, with no buildings and very little organisational structure to assume as a starting point, let alone to maintain. It was all too well aware of its difference from the inherited 'first space' of Judaism, and was often focused on how to negotiate its position in relation to the synagogue – in Jerusalem as well as among the Diaspora Jewish settlements of the wider Roman Empire.[87] In many of these places, maintaining the Jewish tradition *was* an issue, and this frequently led to clashes with the early missionaries.[88]

In addition, the early Christian band is pictured as being continually on the move. This is clearly evident in Luke's missionary narrative, the Acts of the Apostles, which is structured around the movement of the good news out from Jerusalem, through Judea and Samaria, and on 'to the ends of the earth' (Acts 1:8). Earlier in the timeframe, though, it is also true of the gospel material. Indeed, it can be argued that the missionary mentality of the early disciples would have been shaped by their formative experience of the itinerant ministry of Jesus, in which they were apprenticed for three years. It seems that they were continually on the move.[89]

Mark catches this picture well in the early part of his gospel. In chapter 1, for example, he describes Jesus' hectic work of healing and exorcism, partly as a way of illustrating what Jesus meant when he said that 'the kingdom of God has come near' (v. 15). This first day in the public ministry of Jesus is packed with incident – so much so that, at the end of it, his disciples brought many 'who were sick or possessed with demons' for Jesus to heal (v. 32). He clearly hadn't been able to deal with all who had come to seek help from him. Yet early next morning, Jesus leaves to get away to pray. His disciples eventually find him and say to him, 'Everyone is searching for you' and Jesus replies, 'Let us go on to the neighbouring towns, so that I may proclaim the message there also; for that is what I came out to do' (vv. 37–38). The word is out but it needs to go on being spoken to people who have not yet heard it, and this will involve movement.

It is not surprising, therefore, that the New Testament understanding of church involved a commitment to what we have been calling 'second-space' strategies. The good news had to be heard in places it had not been heard before. It is not surprising, either, that the evolving patterns of church leadership were geared towards mission. We read, for example, of the church leadership at Antioch commissioning Paul and Barnabas, under the guidance of the Holy Spirit, to take the gospel further west (Acts 13:1–3). We also read of the Jerusalem Council approving and supporting the movement of the gospel beyond Jewish boundaries into the Gentile world (15:13–29).

The example of Peter's speech at the Jerusalem Council is profoundly important in many ways, not least because it illustrates the 'missionary' dimension of someone we might have described as being primarily a pastor. Was Peter supporting a growing movement simply because he felt he had to, or was there more to it than this? I want to suggest that the latter is the case.

Pastoral leadership involves leadership in mission

Ideas associated with pastoral ministry have become so entwined with 'first space' models of ministry that we are often unable to think beyond these models. 'Pastoral' means 'feeding' and 'pastoring' the flock; it means looking after the congregation – and at one level this is absolutely right. The flock of God needs to be nurtured, taught and cared for, just as sheep are nurtured by their shepherd, and the New Testament says that this ministry is to be undertaken under the guidance of the chief shepherd, Jesus himself (1 Peter 5:4).

However, we may need to revisit the biblical material in order to recover a vital lost dimension, for the New Testament passages on pastoral ministry build upon Old Testament roots (supremely Ezekiel 34), which were fulfilled in the life and ministry of Jesus Christ (the 'chief shepherd'). These models would have been formative in the disciples' minds as they saw Jesus at work and began later to shape their own ministries.

In Ezekiel 34, the word of the Lord comes to Ezekiel concerning the contemporary 'shepherds' (or teachers) of Israel. That word condemns them forthrightly for failing to do what God has asked of them. God's expectations are described in different ways in the course of the prophecy, but an intrinsic part of what the shepherds of Israel were called to do was to 'bring back the strayed' and 'search for the lost' (v. 4, also vv. 6, 8). Because of their abject failure to do this, the Lord says that he himself will come and search for the lost and gather them together: 'I will seek the lost, and I will bring back the strayed, and I will bind up the injured, and I will strengthen the weak, but the fat and the strong I will destroy' (v. 16).

When we turn to the New Testament fulfilment of this vision, it is no surprise that we find it in the life and ministry of Jesus himself. It is particularly striking that when the gospel writers describe Jesus in the role of shepherd or pastor, he is seen to be not only doing the work of teaching and feeding the flock (for example, Mark 6:34–44) but also searching for the lost. In fact, in instances where the imagery of the shepherd is to the fore, this seeking after the lost is the dominant thought.

Luke 15:1–7 is a striking example. The story starts with Jesus being criticised by the Pharisees and teachers of the law for pursuing and concentrating his ministry outside 'the church' (by eating with and welcoming 'sinners', vv. 1–2). Jesus tells the three parables that follow (about the lost sheep, the lost coin and the lost son) precisely in order to justify this activity. His main point is that he is searching out those who are lost because, by doing so, he is mirroring God's great concern for them. In fact, Jesus is openly implying that, through his own actions in the present, God is fulfilling his promise through Ezekiel that he himself would come and search for the lost (Ezekiel 34:16).

Jesus, the 'shepherd', is strikingly pictured as one who *leaves* the 99 (the 'church', as it were) in order to search for the sheep that is lost. It is pretty clear that Jesus is echoing the Ezekiel passage here, and that Luke is underlining the connection by the vocabulary that he uses. The Greek word for 'the lost' in Luke 15:4 is the same word used in the Greek translation of Ezekiel 34:4. It occurs again in Luke 19:10, where Jesus describes the role of the Son of Man as one who 'came to seek out and to save the lost'.[90] Both occasions show that the missionary aspect of pastoring is embedded in the roots of apostolic understanding and practice.

In a similar way, among the 'I am' sayings in John's gospel is the one where Jesus describes himself as the 'good shepherd' (10:11, 14). The story in which it occurs describes Jesus as both 'gate' and 'shepherd' for the sheep, and his role has many implications, but notice in verse 16 that this flock is still in the making. 'I have other sheep that do not belong to this fold', says Jesus. 'I must bring them also, and they will listen to my voice. So there will be one flock, one shepherd.' It is clear from the context that these 'other sheep' are Gentiles, and that part of Jesus' shepherding (or pastoral) ministry was to gather these chosen ones from the nations in order to establish God's worldwide flock under his overall care.

I suspect that this missionary aspect of pastoral ministry also lies behind Paul's words to Timothy in 2 Timothy 4:5. I have often wondered why Timothy was called to 'do the work of an evangelist' if he was basically a pastor. Did the church in Ephesus lack this specific gifting, so Paul asked Timothy to 'double up' and do the work of an evangelist as well as his other duties? I doubt this. If what we have been saying about the biblical role of the pastor makes sense, then Timothy's pastoral ministry would have included the aspect of 'seeking the lost' that gives sense to Paul's words. Part of what it means for Timothy to be a pastor, and to 'carry out your ministry fully', says Paul, is for him to 'do the work of an evangelist' (and, by doing so, to equip others to engage in this ministry too: see Ephesians 4:11–12).

The picture beginning to emerge from these passages is that there is both an overlap and an interrelationship between these two roles. They are not discrete activities, as some today might lead us to think: 'I'm a pastor; you're an evangelist. I'm about building up the church; you are about reaching those outside.' It is certainly fruitless – and quite unbiblical – to play them off against each other. They are mutually supportive activities for the sake of the kingdom and the world.

Developing a 'third space'

What about the 'third space'? What is it, and what might it mean for our approach to evangelism and church mission? In the remainder of this chapter, I want to look at Paul's letter to the Ephesians in order to introduce the idea of a 'third space'. We'll then look at a more contemporary example of 'third-space' thinking and draw some conclusions for evangelism.

The letter to the Ephesians sets out the glorious vision and all-embracing scope of God's missionary purposes for the world. It paints in cosmic terms the enormous riches and benefits of his grace and traces the sheer size of God's plan in Jesus Christ 'to gather up all things in him, things in heaven and things on earth' (1:10), and so bring the whole of creation to its intended goal.

Paul was writing this letter to a group of Gentiles who, by the standards of contemporary Jewish expectation, were second-class citizens because they were not born into God's covenant people – and many of them no doubt felt it. How, then, would God bring about his purposes? Paul actually highlights the 'us' and 'them' problem at various points, not least by the way in which he uses the language of 'we' and 'you'. The first half of chapter 1 is character-ised by the repeated use of 'we' sentences, 'we' being the ones on whom all the blessings of God's riches have been poured. The overriding impression is one of covenantal privilege, emphasised by verse 12, where Paul says that 'we, who were the first to set our hope on Christ, might live for his praise and glory'. He is referring to the Jewish covenantal people, of whom he himself is a member.

This sense of the distinctiveness of the Jewish inheritance is under-lined in chapter 2, where Paul starts referring to the Ephesians as 'you' and points out their alienation from all that he has been talking about. 'You were dead through... trespasses and sins,' he begins (v. 1), and concludes the section by telling his readers:

> Remember that at one time you Gentiles by birth, called 'the uncircumcision' by those who are called 'the circumcision' – a physical circumcision made in the flesh by human hands – remember that you were at that time without Christ, being aliens from the commonwealth of Israel, and strangers to the covenants of promise, having no hope and without God in the world.
> EPHESIANS 2:11–12

Of course, Paul's aim is quite the reverse of exclusion, but the way he sets this distinction up is quite pointed and deliberate. The Ephesian readers might have expected Paul to tell them that, in order to be included properly in all he has been talking about, they need to become like him. They need to make a movement away from where they are and into the proper territory of faith. 'Come over to us,' he seems to be suggesting. There is a 'first-space' expectation about where the power lies and what the Ephesian Gentiles need to do about it.

But Paul is not wanting to take this line for one moment. Like every good communicator, he is skilfully building up the tension in order to deliver the punchline. And what a punchline it is! It involves a rejection of 'first-space' assumptions altogether. Since the coming of Jesus the Messiah, there is no way he can tell them to 'come over to us'. No, both he and they are now called into a new place, for the atoning death of Jesus Christ has created a 'third space' that neither Paul nor his readers naturally occupy. How has it been created? Paul says that it is created because of God's dazzling initiative in Jesus Christ:

> [Christ] is our peace; in his flesh he has made both groups into one and has broken down the dividing wall, that is, the hostility between us. He has abolished the law with its commandments and ordinances, that he might create in himself one new humanity in place of the two, thus making peace, and might reconcile both groups to God in one body through the cross, thus putting to death that hostility through it.
> EPHESIANS 2:14–16

The invitation to enter this 'third space' did not originate with Paul. He may have been the messenger but Paul emphasises that it was Jesus who 'came and proclaimed peace to you who were far off and peace to those who were near; for through him both of us have access in one Spirit to the Father' (vv. 17–18).

Vincent Donovan and 'third-space' thinking

A contemporary missionary whose experience mirrors a similar resolution between inherited first- and second-space approaches to mission is Vincent J. Donovan. His book *Christianity Rediscovered: An epistle from the Masai* has rightly become a classic since its first publication in 1978 and charts Donovan's experience as a Catholic missionary working in Tanzania among the Masai people in the late 1960s and early 1970s. His experience very much reflects the paradox of the modern missionary movement – of second space initiatives ending up as incarnations of first space strategy.

The hub of the missionary settlement to which Donovan went was the mission station, which had four 'well-run, well-looked after, expensive, nonaided schools', a 'small chapel' and 'a hospital, extremely well-built, fairly well-attended, bringing in some mission revenue'. Donovan writes that he became increasingly frustrated at the 'come and see' mentality with which the Catholic Mission was operating, and began to yearn for something more radical. He wrote to his bishop in May 1966, wondering if he 'could make some comments on the mission'. Despite the riches of the resources available, 'the best way to describe realistically the state of this Christian mission is the number zero. As of this month, in the seventh year of this mission's existence, there are no adult Masai practising Christians.' Donovan continued, 'I suddenly feel the urgent need to cast aside all theories and discussions, all efforts at strategy – and simply go to these people and do the work among them for which I came to Africa.' He simply wanted to 'talk to them about God and the Christian message'. 'I know this is a radical departure from traditional procedure,' he went on, 'but I would like to try. I have no theory, no plan, no strategy, no gimmicks – no idea of what will come. I feel rather naked. I will begin as soon as possible.'[91]

This divine prompting launched Donovan into a life-changing exploration of mission and culture as he set out as an evangelist to the Masai. As he gave himself to the task of trying to communicate the gospel in categories that the Masai could grasp and claim for themselves, not only were his own inherited categories challenged but he was also forced to rethink his faith from the ground up, leading to a fresh and deeper understanding, engaging both mind and imagination. Reflecting on the radical change that this required of the patterns of mission that he had inherited, he was later to write, 'The command to go out and preach the gospel has become subtly transformed into "Stay here, take care of what you have. Let others come to you." Missionary movement comes to a dead stop.'[92]

Third-space evangelism?

When *Christianity Rediscovered* was republished in 1982, Vincent Donovan included in its preface some words by a young American student in response to a reading of the book in its original edition. They are quoted at the start of this chapter.[93] Donovan himself describes these words not only as 'good missionary advice' but 'a beautiful description of the unpredictable process of evangelisation, a process leading to that new place where none of us has ever been before'.[94]

They are a brilliant example of what I have been describing as 'third-space' evangelism. Third-space evangelism is a movement away from ourselves towards others, and then a movement with others towards something that is new for both of us. This will involve a fresh recognition that although we may be the messengers in the ministry of evangelism, it is Jesus himself who extends the invitation. Our evangelistic conversations are therefore not two-way, but three-way, with Jesus as the unseen but real presence. The evangelistic invitation is not one in which we say, 'Come to us.' Rather, it is one in which Jesus says to both of us, 'Come to me.' This will involve change for the other person, of course, as the gospel sheds its light on current circumstances and future possibilities, but it will also involve change for me. It involves the recognition that, in evangelism, I too am being drawn nearer to Jesus Christ, and I will be changed in the process.

First-space thinking says, in effect, 'I have the truth; come over to where I am.' Third-space thinking says, 'Come with me. Let's go together. We are both being drawn into a new place, the place where Christ is.'

Third-space church?

The 'third-space' principle extends to the wider understanding of church as well, for Paul's message in Ephesians is corporate as much as individual. This may mean that the form of church that we know is not as central to God's plans as we thought it was, or at least not in the form that it presently takes. The church is not the mover and shaker in mission: God is. As the great German theologian Jürgen Moltmann puts it, 'What we have to learn is not that the church "has" a mission, but the very reverse: that the mission of Christ creates its own church. Mission does not come from the church; it is from mission and in the light of mission that the church has to be understood.'[95]

Some of the assumptions of 'first-space' thinking must be faced honestly. The church is not the controlling agency from which evangelistic forays are made. Rather, the church needs to recover the sense that it is on the move, seeking by the Spirit to respond to God's missionary initiatives with prayerful discernment and risky action. This will mean – as it did in New Testament times – that new forms of church, in unreached contexts, will come into existence as expressions of God's mission.

Where to start? Vincent Donovan's testimony involves the language of conversion – a God-given change of mind and attitude in the light of the circumstances that faced him. The first step was to ask the right question: are people outside the congregation of the faithful being reached with the good news of Jesus? The second step was to recognise that when our organisational structures inhibit mission, action is required. The third was the venture of faith: 'I would like to try,' Donovan said, even though 'I feel rather naked.' And the fourth step is the ongoing adventure of being caught up in the missionary purposes of God, into that third space, wherever it may lead us.

Questions

- Why do you think first-space evangelism has dominated thinking about evangelism over the last 100 years?

- In what ways is third-space evangelism different to second-space? Can you give some local examples?

- What might it take to move your church from first- and second-space to third-space practices?

Part 2

Evangelism and the local church

7

Why we need fishing nets, not safety nets

David Male

The other day, I spoke to a friend who is a church leader; he had recently attended a major church planting conference. He told me that one church planter was lauded from the conference platform for the amazingly quick growth of his new church plant. Throughout the conference, attention kept returning to what a fantastic job he had done and how the church was growing dramatically. The implicit message was simple: 'You should all strive to be like him. If only you could get your church to grow like his.' Later, the same friend had an opportunity to talk individually with this leader and asked how many of the people who had joined his church had no prior connection with church. My friend was shocked by the answer: not a single one!

Clearly some big questions need to be asked about such 'growth', particularly if it represents people who are simply fed up with their own churches and have transferred to something new and exciting. Is this really growth, or simply an example of rearranging the deckchairs on the Titanic? The need is for churches that are not simply providing safety nets for those already in church, but are learning what it means to be genuine fishers of people in this present generation. We need effective evangelising churches that are able to connect the gospel of Jesus to their local communities and become the disciple-makers that the great commission calls us to be.

I am not saying that we should not be concerned about those from a Christian background who may move from one church to another for valid reasons, or may have given up going to church for some time. Figures suggest that there are many in the latter category, and it is good that they are being drawn back into church attendance. But we need to understand our present situation and what is required of us. The vast majority of people have no church connection or background. I have already mentioned the research commissioned by Tearfund in 2007, which suggested that 66 per cent of the UK adult population were not intending to go to any church, however exciting or relevant it might be. The largest proportion of this group was made up of younger people. The research of Sylvia Mayo Collins and others[96] suggests that young people are benignly indifferent to the Christian faith. They might not have the antagonism of their parents' generation, but they see faith as irrelevant for daily life. Most young people, therefore, place their faith in the 'trinity' of family, friends and self. The church does not even get a look in.

I find that a sporting image helps to convey what has happened. It is as if we no longer have a 'home' ground: all our matches are now 'away' games. This is a very different situation from what the church has been familiar with in previous generations. It requires of us very different attitudes, strategies and actions. We used to send missionaries to foreign countries where people had very little contact with or knowledge of the Christian story. Now we are in a similar situation in our own country. If your local church were to send a missionary to plant a church in South-East Asia and they started something that looked very much like your home church, what would you think? It would be crazy in an overseas missionary situation, yet we are in danger of continuing to replicate a church that is not connecting with the majority of the population in our own country. Some churches that are held up as great examples of growth are actually masking the real issue – the need to create churches that can reconnect with people outside. We cannot stay the same and expect the results to be different.

In 2012 the BBC made a documentary called *Reverse Missionaries*, in which leaders of growing churches in the Two-Thirds world came to work with struggling UK churches. Two things repeatedly shocked these leaders from overseas. The first was the cultural shock of realising how little people knew of the Christian story, especially young people. One of the overseas leaders was shown crying on the street after conversations with young people, because they simply knew nothing of the story of Jesus. The second shock was that churches operated only within the church building and were not engaged with their local communities in any meaningful way. On one occasion it was noted that the place where the community gathered in largest numbers was in the pub, which operated as a community centre. One of the visiting leaders asked the church members how many of them were involved with the pub and discovered that no one was: the church seemed to operate in a different universe entirely.

We need more churches that are not content simply to contain the faithful, or only to attract those who are dissatisfied with pro-visions elsewhere. We need to develop churches that can connect with people way outside the orbit of the church. We have more than enough 'safety net' churches for our present numbers. What we need are more 'fishing nets'.

Here are some suggestions of how this might be done. I am not offering a blueprint for how to create an effortlessly successful evangelistic church, but these key issues and principles must be considered carefully if the church is to break out of its own confines and become again a church for all.

Public worship is not the best starting place

One of the first responses of many churches in trying to connect with people outside its walls is to create a new type of church service. They think that what is required is something more family-friendly or more 'relevant' to people who don't normally attend church. But it is vital to understand that the majority are not sitting at home thinking about what their local church could do to attract them on a Sunday. The church and its activities are just not part of their thinking. When we start with church services, we can end up simply drawing in believers who are fed up with their own churches or have become disillusioned about their faith. The base attendance figures might look good but there is, in reality, very little mission or evangelism happening. We have to stop thinking that the answer lies within the church building and understand that the real place to start is out in the community.

Church services are usually the end of the process rather than the beginning. We will look at this process in more detail in the next chapter, but here we can say that it has to start with relationships. Where and how might we, as individuals and as a church, relate to our community? It is out of these developing relationships that stories of faith in Jesus will be naturally shared. Then we can legitimately ask what might be created to help these people become not only hearers of the gospel but also disciples of Jesus. Experience suggests that the process might easily take two to four years: we cannot expect a 'quick hit' to increase numbers at existing services.

There is no return address

One definition of an idiot is someone who keeps doing the same things while expecting different results. I spent 24 hours with some senior church leaders looking at the future of the church. They were all from very different geographical locations and theological backgrounds. I was part of a group in which the first discussion question posed to us asked, 'Why do we need to change?' There was an overwhelming sense that the answer was so obvious, the question did not even require voicing. The group was convinced that we had to look towards the future because the present situation was obviously not connecting the church with its wider local community in an effective manner. We are not calling people back to a golden era but we are moving forward in response to God's leading.

I have been fascinated again by looking at how the early church operated in its evangelistic context. Jesus gave the apostles their vision statement before his ascension. He told them at their final gathering, 'You will receive power when the Holy Spirit has come upon you; and you will be my witnesses in Jerusalem, in all Judea and Samaria, and to the ends of the earth' (Acts 1:8).

The church then began in the most astonishing manner on the Day of Pentecost, when over 3,000 people were added to the fledgling community. I imagine Peter and the other apostles debriefing after the day, discussing how they must have discovered the definitive model for church growth after such a phenomenal beginning. Everything was set for success. They could write the manual, hone the course materials and produce the DVD, and the triumphs would surely continue. As I visit churches, I often hear Acts 2 used as the basic ground-plan for evangelism and church growth, and yet that is not how the New Testament writers viewed it. The events in Jerusalem did not become the blueprint for church growth, with all future churches becoming like the one in Jerusalem. They were to move out from Jerusalem rather than creating clones of the Jerusalem church throughout the world. There were certain constants required for church but no fixed idea of how it would develop in each context.

Eight years later, Peter had a vision, on a roof top in the port of Joppa, that totally changed his mindset (see Acts 10—11). In the vision, he was presented with all sorts of animals that, as a good Jew, he was not allowed to eat or even touch, and was told by God to kill and eat them. At the same time, an Italian soldier who was not a follower of Jesus had a vision in which he was told to make contact with Peter. The fascinating scenario that ensues sees Peter going to Cornelius' house in the port of Caesarea. According to Jewish regulations, he was not meant to be in the same house as Gentiles, but his vision had convinced him that 'God has shown me that I should not call anyone profane or unclean' (10:28).

Peter realised through this experience that God was not calling every church to replicate the one at Jerusalem but that the shape of the church would adapt to the local conditions as the evangelism continued into more of the known world. Jesus' vision statement does not call us back to a single design but leads us instead on an adventure to discover what might be created in different localities as the gospel takes root and begins to grow. This was certainly the experience of Peter – and then Paul – as the gospel moved into Gentile areas. At each stage they were faced with important cultural issues which demanded fresh thinking about what it meant for new believers to become, and then live as, disciples of Jesus.

I find it very interesting that Luke gives so much space to his account of Peter's transformative experience with Cornelius. As a result of it, Peter learnt the importance of looking at the everyday with new eyes, with *God's* eyes, and this meant that he saw the familiar in a radically different way. The church could never be the same, and the gospel began to spread to the ends of the known world through the ministry of Paul. Much of the rest of the New Testament deals with the issues of what the church was to look like in these changing situations. The challenge for us, as it was for the first Christians, is not about getting people back to what we presume is 'proper' church; it means trying to understand how people's own situations might become church. We cannot return to the golden days of church life (if they ever existed); nor can we necessarily preserve everything that we love.

I love planning and strategy but, as I have studied the book of Acts, I have been struck by the dynamic interplay between God's activity through his Holy Spirit on the one hand, and the church's response on the other. Not much of the church's early life was based on strategic planning. I see no evidence in the New Testament of the apostles gathering together to discuss how they might evangelise Saul or deciding who might face martyrdom to allow the church to grow. This realisation was summed up for me in the first words of a book I read recently: Acts tells the exciting story of how the Spirit led the early Jesus community to respond creatively and continually in new and surprising situations as it preached the gospel.[97]

Surprising things were happening, and the church had to discover how to react appropriately. It's helpful to be reminded of the central role of the Spirit in helping the church to respond resourcefully: they could not proceed in their evangelism until the Spirit had come upon them. The church continually faced tough questions as it grappled with new situations: what to do about Saul, the hated persecutor of the church who suddenly claimed conversion, or what to do when Gentiles responded to the gospel and were filled with the Holy Spirit. Being involved in evangelism is partly about learning how to respond to God's activity in the Spirit – however surprising and even shocking it might seem to us.

John V. Taylor comments on the unpredictability we face in working with God: 'Mission is often described as if it were the planned extension of an old building. But in fact it has usually been more like an unexpected explosion... we should have had the modesty to recognise that the Breath of God has always played a far more decisive part than our human strategy.'[98] No wonder the book of Acts highlights the importance of prayer for the fledgling church, for it is in prayer that we seek by the Spirit to discern God's activities and ask for his wisdom to know how to respond to what he is doing in his surprising and often explosive ways.

We plant the gospel and the church grows: this order is important

We do not plant a church from which to evangelise; we evangelise and see a church take shape as God works. This order is vital so that the resulting embryonic church reflects both the gospel and the people who are becoming Jesus' disciples. It must be both 'free' and 'rooted' – 'rooted' in the gospel and reflecting this clearly in the way the community lives out its faith, but 'free' in the sense that it is shaped by the people and the context in which it is planted. We need to learn from Peter that we are not aiming to reproduce previous forms of church (however good they may be), but to sow the gospel and then wait to see what kind of local church emerges. It is much more like church planting in foreign and unknown lands than simply copying the latest successful model of church growth that we might have read or heard about.

This new viewpoint might change us

One of the earliest lessons I learned about evangelism was that although we rightly concentrate on seeing other people's lives changed, we ourselves will be changed through the experience of sharing our faith. That was certainly what happened to Peter and many of the early church leaders. We may encounter a number of these moments in our own lives, when we are challenged to think again about our understandings of God and the gospel. When we meet and get to know other people who do not think as we do, we may find that our assumptions are challenged, our theology stretched and our limitations exposed. Recently I have got to know some of those involved in the 'Occupy' movement. Listening to them has challenged my caricatured picture of them and forced me to reflect on the heart of the gospel.

It takes courage to allow the gospel to work in us as well as in others. When we planted the Net Church in Huddersfield, I discovered that my assumptions and ideas were being radically challenged. We were often stretched as we reflected on what church was for, and how our practices of church were being shaped by our evangelism and by those who were discovering Jesus for themselves.

At that time, I was struck by these words from John's gospel, 'Very truly, I tell you, unless a grain of wheat falls into the earth and dies, it remains just a single grain; but if it dies, it bears much fruit' (12:24). This pattern of dying to live, as seen in our baptism, challenges us to ask what we will allow to die so that other things can flourish and become more fruitful. Which practices are merely cultural preferences rather than gospel imperatives? What are we willing to sacrifice for the sake of the gospel? What might God be asking us to let go?

Welcome the three eccentrics

Who are the Philips, Corneliuses and Pauls in your local context? This may not be a question that you have pondered greatly, but it is an important one.

Is there space for the Philips – those who want to do something prompted by God that seems a bit crazy? In Acts 8, after preaching in Samaria, Philip responds to the Spirit's calling and waits by the road from Jerusalem to Gaza. Then he tries to hitch a ride on a passing chariot. I wonder how much of our sensible pragmatism squeezes such people out of our churches. Of course they need to be accountable, but will we support them as they follow God's leading? Will we trust them to respond to the unpredictable promptings of the Spirit?

Who might be the Corneliuses in your locality? I was part of a small group involving a number of bishops recently, and I asked this question. Who are the people who do not belong to the church but have something to say to us that might be from God? I have found such people working in a hotel, running a school or simply being a key figure in the local neighbourhood. Where are those whom God has been preparing to help us, guide us or challenge us, and how would we know them if we met them?

Finally, who might be the Pauls in your situation? These are the people who want to do things differently. They might not be the easiest to work with, but they have a clear calling and a sense of adventure. They want to get on and try things out, and they will probably not proceed in the way you would.

The danger for those of us who are leaders is that we look for people in our churches who fit in easily and are satisfied with the present structures. But our present missionary situation challenges us to search for the three eccentrics, to take us to new places for the sake of the gospel. They might not represent the safe options and their plans may not always work out successfully, but they are worth the investment. The issue for the church is how to keep them from being 'tamed', becoming acquiescent to our demands. They need to be rooted in the gospel but allowed to remain risk-takers. In this new day of the mission field, we desperately need to find these people, but they often remain on the margins of our churches, disillusioned by the status quo and frustrated by the 'sameness' and 'safety' around them. Will we have the courage to release them?

The challenge of discipleship

We will look at the challenge of discipleship in greater depth in chapter 9, because this is a vital area for us to think about. The issue we face is not how to get more people into church or even the most effective ways to help them make a decision to follow Jesus, but how to enable them to become mature and vivid disciples of Jesus. How – using Paul's words – do we help people to come 'to maturity, to the measure of the full stature of Christ' (Ephesians 4:13)? In the past, the prevailing culture helped with this process. Most people knew the Christian story, had experience of the church and were part of a society that upheld traditional Christian values and ethics. Often, coming to faith reignited beliefs that were already latent. Now, we may see people exploring spirituality, but it is often coupled with confusion or ignorance about the Christian faith. How do we help them not only make a decision about Jesus but also be transformed by him so that they become agents of transformation for others?

We reflect the pattern of Jesus' life

Sometimes, when I have raised these issues at Christian gatherings, I have been accused of pandering to the prevailing hedonistic culture or selling out to a consumer lifestyle. People comment that it sounds like creating church the way people want it, or dumbing down the gospel and making evangelism too palatable. But I think that Jesus' life shows us a pattern that helps us see the full picture of how the church must respond in our present times. We can see it in the following three ways.

His birth and life

First, we have to enter the world fully. This is where Jesus began his ministry to us – by entering our world. He became human and embraced earthly life in first-century Palestine. We must start by living in the world God has given to us, maybe stepping out of our comfort zones so that we enter more fully the life of our local communities in all its aspects. This is the message of Jesus' incarnation.

His death

Second, we are to live in this world counterculturally. The cross reminds us that, at present, the world is not as it should be. Perhaps the greatest challenge for the gospel today is not scientific rationalism or the strident atheism of Richard Dawkins and others, but consumerism, which has its own idols, places of worship, liturgy, evangelists and discipleship courses. The gospel calls us and those who become disciples to live differently in the face of this huge challenge. We can no longer fit in with the assumptions of our age or expect to fit Jesus into its lifestyle. Jesus made this clear to the crowds that followed him: 'If any want to become my followers, let them deny themselves and take up their cross and follow me' (Mark 8:34). Consumerism does not sit well with self-denial and sacrifice.

It is important to recognise the example that Jesus' life gives to us. Too often, the church and Christians insist on being countercultural without having truly developed relationships and fully entered the communities around them. If we don't hold these two elements together, we are easily perceived as those who condemn and judge, simply shouting from the sidelines.

His resurrection

As we know, the story of Jesus does not end at the cross. There is a world to come, which we eagerly anticipate. Jesus' resurrection reminds us that our world is not the final story but that God will have the last word. Paul sums this up in Romans 8:18, when he writes, 'I consider that the sufferings of this present time are not worth comparing with the glory about to be revealed in us.' We are called to be signposts and tasters of what is yet to come, of a world with no sorrow, pain or tears. This does not mean that we abandon the present world, but we seek to transform it, in our own lives and the lives of our communities. By doing so, we convey something of the perfection that is to come, which has already been set in motion by the cross, resurrection and coming of the Spirit.

In April 2010, a man set out to sail his boat from Gillingham to Southampton, although he had no experience of sailing. He needed first to sail down the River Medway to reach the sea. He calculated that upon reaching this point, all he had to do was to turn right and hug the coast and he would eventually arrive safely in the port of Southampton. Unfortunately he did not realise that there was a small island – the Isle of Sheppey – just where the river met the sea. Having reached the sea, he followed his plan of hugging the coast, but the presence of the island meant that he simply sailed round it, again and again. He did this three times before he was rescued by the coastguards. They suggested that next time it might be easier and safer for him to take the train.

I sometimes feel that we are like that novice sailor. We too easily hug the coast, wanting to keep in sight what is recognisable and well known. In these present times, however, I suspect that God is calling us to leave the safety of familiar shores and cast off into deeper waters. It may mean we are less sure of where we are going, and the way may be less easy to navigate, but we believe that this is where we must go and that God is calling us to step out. It will be daunting and uncertain at times, but we should remember Jesus' words to his disciples as we venture out, just as they did: 'Remember, I am with you always, to the end of the age' (Matthew 28:20).

Questions

- Would you agree with the conclusion that all our games are now 'away' games?

- How might this impact the way you do 'church'?

- If public worship is not the best starting place for evangelism, what might be?

- What do you think is the relationship between worship and evangelism?

8

Finding your voice as a leader in evangelism

David Male

The 2010 film *The King's Speech*, which won three Oscars, was an uplifting story of the British King George VI, who 'found his voice' in the face of the nation's desperate need for leadership after the abdication of his brother, Edward VIII. The film beautifully portrays the tale of a reluctant leader who, hampered by shyness and a speech impediment, realised that he would nevertheless have to become king. He faced certain requirements if he was to discharge his duties to the best of his abilities. He not only had to overcome his speech problem but had to grow in confidence so that he could become the leader needed for the critical times that Britain was facing.

We need church leaders, both paid and volunteers, who are 'finding their voice' when it comes to leading their churches in evangelism. We live in times when fewer people are seeing church as normal or relevant and the old ways of doing church no longer have the same impact, so we need leaders who will lovingly and patiently lead their churches in this crucial area. I do not think I can overemphasise the responsibility of church leaders in modelling this task, both through their own lives and by equipping others, so that church members can be more effective witnesses in their communities. This is probably the most important single factor in getting the word out.

I spend much of my working life with church leaders and those training to be church leaders. Often, when we talk together about evangelism, there is a sense of embarrassment, either because they personally find evangelism so difficult or because church activities and time spent with church people have come to dominate their lives. LICC consulted 150 church leaders after the launch of its 'Imagine' project in 2003. Its findings clearly show that leaders struggle with time pressures, work–life balance and long working hours. Whatever their own wishes or gifting in evangelism, the 'black hole' of church life continually holds them back and makes them feel helpless, guilty and frustrated. The report commented that leaders 'had a growing sense that we have looked for security in church structures, programmes, plans and vision statements, neglecting the transforming power of the Spirit of Jesus Christ engaged in the lives of "ordinary" Christians; people who carry the presence of God into their daily context.'[99]

We need to recognise that not all church leaders – perhaps not even the majority – are natural evangelists. Many leaders have come into church leadership because of their pastoral or teaching gifts. A piece of research named 'Apprentice' – carried out in 2009 as part of the 'Imagine' project – surveyed 3,000 people at Spring Harvest. It revealed that only 47% of people in any leadership capacity knew how to 'lead someone to Christ'. The figure for paid leaders was 71%. It also showed that only 56% of people in any leadership capacity felt they had a story to tell about how God had worked in their life. The figure for paid leaders on the same issue was 69%.[100] In my experience, if the key leaders in the church are not promoting and practising evangelism, it will not become a high priority for the congregation as a whole. It will become, once again, a side activity for the people who are 'into' it or are specialists in the area.

If, as a leader, you don't see yourself as an evangelist and don't feel you can lead from the front, is it perhaps possible to lead from the back or middle? What does it mean to be a local evangelistic church leader for the sake of the world when you are not a natural evangelist?

The apostle Paul's words to his mentee Timothy can help greatly in finding a constructive way forward. We know that Timothy was a young, timid leader who was leading a church dominated by people with strong egos and personalities, and that the church was deeply divided by various theological disputes. In this situation, Paul writes to Timothy, 'As for you, always be sober, endure suffering, do the work of an evangelist, carry out your ministry fully' (2 Timothy 4:5).

As we saw in chapter 3, the word 'evangelist' is found only three times in the New Testament (Acts 21:8; Ephesians 4:11; 2 Timothy 4:5). In Acts 21 it is used to describe Philip, one of the seven deacons chosen in Acts 6:5, who soon found himself sharing the good news with the Ethiopian eunuch on the road to Gaza (8:26–40). In Ephesians 4, Paul talks about the 'evangelist' as one of the gifts given by God for the sake of the church, in order 'to equip the saints for the work of ministry' (v. 12; that is, enabling others in this context to share the gospel too). But in his second letter to Timothy, Paul uses the term in a slightly different way. He is commanding Timothy to perform his ministry fully as Paul prepares for the end of his own ministry (see 4:6–9). Part of Timothy's work in fulfilling his ministry is to 'do the work of an evangelist'. It's as if Paul is saying to him, 'I know you find this part of your ministry really difficult, but you need to do it for the sake of the gospel and the church. You are not an evangelist like Philip but, in leading your church, you need to act as an evangelist.' We might even say that Paul was urging Timothy to 'find his voice'. He recognises that Timothy will need to be in control of himself ('be sober'), especially of his own fears and perhaps his self-doubt. Paul is realistic about such leadership and recognises that it will not be easy for Timothy. He highlights a number of times in this letter that such ministry will involve suffering (2 Timothy 1:8; 2:2; 3:12).

It is not easy to give evangelism a high priority in the church. Don't try to do it if you want a quiet or easy life! Two leaders from very different backgrounds spoke recently to some of my students about how they had developed significant evangelistic ministries through their churches. I was fascinated to hear in both accounts that there had been a key moment when each of them had had to stand their ground against people in the church who did not want to move in that direction. They agreed that this had been a turning point for them, but that it also came with a significant personal cost, because of the pressure it put on them but also because of the impact it had on other leaders in the church.

I am not saying that, as a leader, you suddenly have to become an evangelistic speaker like Billy Graham, start preaching on street corners, give out tracts to everyone who passes the church, have conversations about God with total strangers or completely change your personality. That would be a false way to 'find your voice'. I believe that God wants to use you as you are; you do not have to become someone you are not. But, to use Paul's words, it does mean thinking about how you can work at the issue under God, in order to lead your church in evangelism whatever your gifts and temperament. Our present situation calls for the church to leave the margins and divest itself of its ghetto mindset – and the leader's role is crucial in this.

How, then, do you lead in evangelism when you might be more comfortable taking a back seat? Here are some principles I have discovered over the years, which might help leaders to think about how they can focus their leadership in evangelism and take responsibility for it, even when they don't see themselves as 'evangelists'. These are tasks that they cannot afford to delegate to others.

Envision

Transformed leaders have a clear conviction that God can and will work through their congregation to change lives and that their congregation of people can be used by God to help change the world. Such vision begins with the clear vision of the evangelising community and what that community might look like in its particular setting and circumstances.[101]

The role of the evangelising leader is to help a congregation understand how it can be involved in God's big story of redemption and salvation. The key is for the church to understand that they exist for the sake of the others who do not yet belong. It is too easy for people to feel instinctively that this is 'their church' and exists to 'feed them'. The wrong question often asked by church members is, 'What am I getting out of this?' I talked to someone at a party recently who had moved to a new town and had started attending the local church, near her new house. She was beginning to wonder if it really was the right place for her because the sermons were nowhere near as good as they had been in her previous church. I gently suggested that, as she had been a Christian for over 20 years, good sermons might not need to be her first priority. Perhaps the issue was whether this was the place where she could fulfil God's mission in her new setting. A better question to ask might be, 'How might I better serve God and my new community in this place?'

When I planted the Net Church in Huddersfield in 1999, I realised within the first year that the envisioning process was the most crucial role for me as a leader. It was therefore the task to which I had to devote my best energy, creativity and attention. I aimed to say to the congregation every month, in a variety of different ways, 'Remember why we are here: it is to connect unchurched people to Jesus, and there is nothing more exciting than this.' Envisioning may be the most significant role of any leader seeking to do the work of an evangelist. I was astounded by how quickly people lost the vision and started thinking about internal matters. That's why leaders must keep the process of envisioning regular, creative and innovative. Doing it only once a year, or even occasionally, is never enough. It can easily sound repetitive, so we have to be inventive in how, where and when we do it, but we have to do it! Rick Warren uses the concept of the 'Nehemiah Principle', which is based on the leadership of Nehemiah in helping the nation of Israel to rebuild the walls of Jerusalem. He says, 'Vision and purpose must be restated every 26 days to keep the church moving in the right direction.'[102]

I remember being part of the leadership team of a largish church that caused me endless frustrations. I might have said we had no vision at all, but it would be more honest to say that we had about 200 different and contradictory visions. Without a *shared* vision, lots of good people were working energetically at their own visions, but this had the effect of dramatically diffusing the energy of the church as a whole. I came away from that experience vowing that I would never again be part of a church that had no clear sense of where it was going and was not communicating to each person in the church how they could be part of the vision.

Of course, it may not be the church that has lost the vision for evangelism. It might be the leaders themselves. The sense of purpose has gone, or the years have dulled the reality of the good news for them. One of the findings of LICC's 'What the Leaders Said' consultation was that many leaders were struggling even more than their congregations to live out their faith.[103] If this is your experience, you must find some time and support from others, and (as the apostle John puts it) discover again your 'first love' (Revelation 2:4). As leaders, we need to keep alive a strong sense of God's love for us and his transforming work in our lives. This must always be the basis of our ministry as leaders in evangelism. Everything about 'doing the work of an evangelist' must arise from our own living experience of God. This is why our spiritual disciplines are so important in keeping our encounter with God alive and fresh. The busyness of church life can easily dull the vibrancy of our relationship with God. Evangelism cannot be allowed to remain simply another item on an agenda.

Encourage

To 'do the work of an evangelist' means encouraging people in their evangelism as individuals and as a community. One of our favourite phrases at the church in Huddersfield was 'minimise meetings and maximise relationships'. You can't ask people to be always at church events and then wonder why they have so few relationships with people outside church. As leaders, we may have to rethink how we view those under our care. Often we think that the really good members are those who come to all the services and meetings we organise. Whether or not people are supporting what the church does becomes the most important measure of our effectiveness as ministers. Perhaps we need to ask some other types of questions, such as 'How do we spend our time when we are not at church?'

Another great way to encourage individuals is to take them or send them away on mission elsewhere. One of the best things we ever did in Huddersfield was to send ten people to Taiwan to be involved in mission with a church we had partnered. Some of these people were new Christians, and for them to see what God was doing on the other side of the world was mindblowing. To be involved in intensive periods of mission can be a life-changing opportunity.

One of the best practical tools I have used to help people really get in touch with those outside church is to take a questionnaire out to public areas and engage with passers-by. The questionnaire we use (which came from the Arrow Leadership Course) is designed as a listening exercise for leaders and churches. It asks questions like:

- If you were asked by a teenager, 'What is life all about?', how would you respond?
- When life has been hard on you, where do you turn for help?
- Do you pray? If so, who do you think you are praying to?

The initiative is designed to help leaders and church members reconnect with people outside the church by listening to what they say. The aim is not to have long conversations with them or even to use the exercise as a form of evangelism, but simply to understand what men and women on local streets are thinking and feeling about faith and the church. I find it really helps church members to reconnect with those who are way outside the church. They often gain a new understanding not only of what people are thinking, but also of what it means to feel lost. Finally, people on the street are often amazed to discover that the church genuinely wants to hear their thoughts. I have used these questionnaires with church leaders and students to great effect. I also know that the leaders have found the experience so beneficial that they have then used them with their own congregations.

Equip

I remember the evangelist J. John telling a conference how he had surveyed about 1,000 churches where he had been invited to speak evangelistically about the level of training they gave their members. Clearly, the fact that these churches had invited an evangelist showed some level of evangelistic initiative and enthusiasm, but the survey responses showed that only 36 churches had provided any specific training for members. No wonder we are struggling in our evangelism as a church! People are often inhibited because they feel that they don't know what to do. We are probably not doing enough to allay their fears and provide them with necessary skills to share their faith with others.

We have to consider not only the forms of our training but exactly what we are asking people to do in evangelism and how we might encourage church members who find the whole area difficult or daunting. In Huddersfield we asked ourselves as a leadership team some strategic questions about evangelism in the church. The main question was, 'Are we expecting every member of the church to be able to share their faith in such a way that they will be able to lead another person to faith in Christ?' Many of the major evangelism training courses assume that this is the goal, regardless of the personality or gifting of its members. After much discussion, we decided that this was not a realistic prospect for every person in the church. Certainly some could do it, but for many it seemed too massive an expectation and might even cause them simply to give up and do nothing. So we worked on a kind of 'contract' with our members, arriving at three straightforward things we were asking everyone in the church to do if they followed Jesus. It was only one aspect of our outreach, but a foundational one.

- First, we asked them to pray. We felt that any Christian could and should be praying regularly for their friends, neighbours, workmates and family members who did not know Christ. We asked everyone and they all felt that this was something they could do, so we produced aids such as bookmarks and encouraged small groups to be praying for specific people.

- Second, we asked them to tell their story. Again we felt that everyone should be able to explain how they had met Jesus and what difference he was making to their lives. We found that some people needed some help with this, so we regularly held short training courses for them.[104]

- Lastly, we asked them to invite people. We felt that everyone should be able to invite people to the events that we organised as a church. We put on a wide variety – from social gatherings to evangelistic evenings – promising to create events to which we felt people would feel proud to bring their friends. We worked very closely with church members to ensure that the occasions were high-quality and relevant for their friends. As a result, usually about 50% of people who attended were from outside the church.

It was a simple and clear strategy, and it seemed to work. We also laid on groups to help people who had been brought along by a church friend and now wanted to find out more about the Christian faith. We set up groups such as 'Just Looking' for those who were spiritually curious and a discipleship group for those who were new to the faith. People would often join these groups with the friend from the church community who had initially invited them to an event. We regularly advertised these opportunities and used a simple sign-up form.

As leaders, we need to understand there is a difference between 'telling' and 'training'. Often we think we are training because we talk about the high value of evangelism or preach about the importance of sharing our faith. 'Envisioning' and 'encouraging' must go together with 'equipping', but it is not enough to tell people what to do. We need to model it as well.

Example

Being an example is an imperative for any leader. We must be seen to be taking the lead, even if we are not natural evangelists. I have found that if we are asking people to invite friends to an event, I must be inviting people too. If we are not doing it ourselves, how can we expect anyone else to take part? You may be thinking that you hate doing this or find it difficult. Well, so do your church members! Share these feelings with them, but still give an example.

A key to growing together in this is to share with the church both your successes and your failures in evangelism. You will discover that this gives them permission to try and also permission to fail. Don't just tell them about the friends who accepted invitations or about great conversations you've had about Jesus. Share also those times when people said 'No' to you, occasions when you were too scared or shy to say anything, or times when you had opportunities to tell your story and messed it up. Sharing like this helps to liberate everyone to 'have a go'. If people think you are like them, yet you are still involved in evangelism, they are much more likely to get involved themselves, because they realise that success is dependent on God alone. On the other hand, if you are a gifted evangelist, the danger is that people think they can never be like you, and so they revert to the view that evangelism is only for the expert.

I recently talked to a good friend who said that she was fed up with her church leader always telling the congregation from the front that they should be spending time with people outside the church when she knew he didn't have any such contacts himself. This kind of thing is immensely demotivating.

The biggest hindrance to setting an example is time-pressure. A leader who is called to do the work of an evangelist will need time to develop relationships with those outside the church (other than marriage or baptism couples, whom we meet through our regular work). Often, the clamour from the congregation for a leader's attention means that there is no time left for anyone else. The problem for leaders is that if you don't live by your priorities, you will end up living by your pressures.

Hundreds of young church leaders have told me that one of the driving forces that led them into ministry was a desire to share their faith. Six or seven years into their ministry, though, they rarely see non-churchgoers, let alone get to know such people and develop meaningful relationships with them. This is serious and needs to be dealt with quickly. Church leaders have to take control of their time in order to be available to those outside the church. For myself, a love of sport helps greatly with this. It means that I spend time with lots of different people – whether playing for a local sports team, attending a gym or playing golf – and I have been able to make some lasting and valuable friendships in this way. When I moved to Cambridge to work in a theological college, I discovered that my time for such friendships shrank considerably. So I joined a local football club, where my son plays, and have got to know a wonderful set of lads, for whom I pray regularly. Just recently I had the honour of conducting the marriage of the team's manager, which many of the other players attended. I am also now playing golf with some of the team.

I would suggest that, to do the work of an evangelist, you might need to allocate a day a week to spending time with people outside the church. This might involve doing an activity you enjoy with others, spending time in a local coffee shop, voluntary work with a non-church organisation, or chaplaincy work in a local supermarket. This puts you in contact with people whom God loves and gives them access to a Christian; it also enables you to learn from people outside church about what they are thinking and how they are living.

You may feel uncomfortable trying to justify the use of a whole day when you are so busy, but it sends a very clear signal to the church about your priorities.

Expectancy

Expectancy is about an awareness that God is at work and delights in using us in his mission. Prayer is at the heart of this increased expectancy as the church becomes more aware of God's power to work and save. Prayer continually reminds all of us that evangelism is God's work, a work in which we cooperate. We are not in control of the process, but prayer is the crucial element in our role, both individually and corporately. If we want to be doing more about getting the word out, we will need to be praying more. As leaders, we will need to consider carefully how we enable the church to pray together, both on a Sunday and during the week. If we are praying together, I find that this leads to an increasing openness to the promptings of the Holy Spirit in evangelism – both for individuals and for the church as a whole. Perhaps someone feels an urge to talk to a certain individual, or the church begins to feel that God is calling it to connect with a certain group in the vicinity.

Love–Relate–Create

I have discovered that churches which create communities that connect with unchurched people often use a very simple method for their evangelism. Its simplicity struck me when I heard two young women talking about how they had come to faith through a new church plant in Cambridge. Neither of them had had an easy life, yet it was obvious that they had been transformed by Jesus and they wanted others to have the same opportunity to discover him. As they spoke to some of my students, I started scribbling notes and realised that they had experienced a very straightforward process. It was simply 'Love–Relate–Create'.

- Love: The process begins when we begin to see others as God sees them, and to care for them as God cares. Our motivation cannot be numbers or growth or success, but simply the love of God that 'compels us', as Paul says (2 Corinthians 5:14, NIV). This is why prayer and our own experience of God are so basic to our evangelism. We cannot manufacture this love; it comes from the experience of God's love for us.

- Relate: One of the things that love does is to send us out to relate to the people around us. It is the eternal pattern expressed in John's famous words, 'For God so loved the world that he sent his only Son' (John 3:16). God's love cannot be contained; it is always wanting to get out. We might relate to others in our street, our neighbourhood, our place of work, the school playground or the local social club. These might all be places we regularly go, but we need to remember that we are called to be there infused with the love of God. I often hear church leaders saying, 'The church doesn't have many connections with the community.' That might be true for the church in its official activities, but through its members it has thousands of contacts every day of the year. The real issue is what we do with these connections, and how the church helps and encourages people with them.

- Create: Loving and relating leads to the question of outcomes for these relationships: what can we create to help the people we love begin to discover God for themselves? It might be as simple as inviting a few friends to gather in a home to eat and talk together about faith. It might mean starting a group for people to discover more about Jesus in the local school, sports club or community centre. It may even be a new kind of church event or service. The possibilities are endless but it is important that they arise out of love and relationship. Only then will something natural and organic begin to emerge.

In church life I often see a movement that is opposite to the one described above. A church wants to create something different –

like a family service, Messy Church or café church – to attract new members. Having started it, they realise that they now need to get people to come along. Only then do they understand the importance of relating to people so that they will come to what has been created. Then, once they have started coming, they need to be cared for. So we see church strategies that look much more like 'Create–Relate–Love' than 'Love–Relate–Create'.

As I listened to those two young women speaking about their experiences, I realised that something else, very profound, was taking place in their church. As they spoke about themselves, I saw that they were following the same pattern in their Christian lives. They talked about being motivated by the love that they had received, so that they were now looking out for mothers in their school playground who seemed to be struggling. They would invite these mothers for coffee, provide a listening ear and offer genuine friendship and support, perhaps offering to pray for them. They also spoke about the possibility of starting a church in their launderette for all the people they were meeting there. They were a living expression of 'Love–Relate–Create'.

Later, I had an enlightening conversation with the leader of their church. She told me that she had seen these women loving people, befriending them, supporting them, praying for them and thinking about how they might express Jesus to them. But she also realised she had never given them any training in pastoral matters, praying for others or evangelism. It dawned on her that their knowledge had been 'caught' rather than 'taught'. Their experience of love and relationships in the church had so captivated them that they naturally reproduced it.

I recently discovered a simple but profound book, *The Art of Neighbouring*, that aims to help church members connect with their neighbours. It begins with the command to love our neighbours, and then asks what that love might look like for those living around us. It encourages us to develop relationships with the people in the eight

houses or flats nearest to us. Jay Pathak, one of the
book, has developed this idea with other church le
Colorado, and is finding that it is having life-changing
only for individuals but for whole communities.[105]

In conclusion, I agree with George Barna's insight into effective
evangelism: 'Pastors must lead and the church must have a plan and
support evangelistic efforts.'[106] Leaders may not be gifted evangelists
but, as I have already stated, if evangelism is to have the highest
priority in their church, they cannot delegate it to others or simply
hope that someone else will do it. Leading doesn't mean being
the key church evangelist but it does require generating a healthy
evangelistic environment in the church, which encourages everyone
to get involved. Coupled with this, there must be a strategy that is
agreed, understood and lived out by the entire congregation. Church
members need to know what is expected of them and how they will
be supported in their evangelistic tasks. All this doesn't just happen:
it needs to be intentional, and will involve careful negotiation
between leadership and church members. It will take time to have
the necessary conversations and to put in place the requisite training
provision. It may also mean that some other church activities cease
in order to give higher priority to the work of evangelism.

Ultimately, the church's evangelistic work must not be considered
as the arena of a few specialists. It has to be viewed as the natural
task of the whole church, with different roles being assigned to
differing kinds of people. Bishop Stephen Cottrell emphasises this
when he comments, 'According to our different personalities, gifts
and circumstances, each of us has a part to play in God's work of
evangelism.'[107]

Questions

- Where are the gifts of evangelism in your leadership team?

- In what ways might you give a vision for evangelism in your congregation?

- What specific training would be appropriate for your congregation to give skills for witness in the whole of life?

- How are you modelling evangelism as a church leader?

9

What's the connection between evangelism and discipleship?

David Male

Is discipleship what happens after evangelism or is evangelism a by-product of discipleship? The answer to this question is crucial to effective evangelism and to developing vision and strategy for the local church.

At my church a student from the local Christian Union told us about their plans for the mission week that was starting the next day. She informed us about all the various events they were organising for the week. At the end of her five-minute slot she added that her role was to be in charge of discipleship following the mission week. She reminded us that It was very important that this was not just considered to be a week's mission, but that contacts were followed up and people who had expressed faith were supported and encouraged. Her final words were that, so far, though, they hadn't made any plans for discipleship after the mission!

This is a very different assessment from that of Dallas Willard, an American philosopher known for his writings on Christian spiritual formation. He concludes, 'We would intend to make disciples and let converts happen rather than intending to make converts and let disciples happen.'[108] I think the emphasis of the New Testament would support his view that evangelism naturally flows from being a disciple of Jesus. The first churches understood that when we live as disciples in the power and presence of the risen Christ, evangelism happens. It is a natural consequence and needs no manufacturing or special gifting. It is simply the outworking of a life lived on the vine with Christ; fruit must follow in us but also through us. This seems to make much more sense of the story of the early church. As Willard helpfully comments, 'It is about being disciples, it is about intentionally making disciples and we must know how to bring people to believe in Jesus as the King.'[109]

As Paul Weston comments in chapter 3, 'What is evangelism?', the New Testament seldom explicitly encourages church members to get out there and evangelise their family, friends and neighbours. The expectation is that evangelism is what naturally happens when you are living your life in Christ. Evangelism is not a specialised activity for just a few experts, but is for everyone as they live out their everyday lives empowered by the risen Jesus.

It's important to understand that the lack of specific commands about evangelism in the New Testament is not because it was not happening in the early church. In fact, the complete opposite was the case, and the early church grew spectacularly across the Roman world. Kenneth Latourette observes about this amazing growth:

> Never in the history of the race has this record ever quite been equalled. Never in so short a time has any other religious faith, or, for that matter, any other set of ideas, religious, political, or economic, without the aid of physical force or of social or cultural prestige, achieved so commanding a position in such an important culture.[110]

David Barrett estimates that there were one million Christians by AD100 and 44 million by AD500.[111] But as you read the New

Testament, you don't see the apostles and early church motivating its members, in the way we often do today, to evangelise. There are no accounts of apostles explicitly telling people they must get out and evangelise all their friends and family. I cannot find any advice given about attending an evangelism training course or that guilt-inducing sense of 'I have to do this'. Yet evangelism was undoubtedly happening everywhere, and the church was growing spectacularly as people came to faith in Jesus.

The last chapter in Graham Tomlin's excellent book *The Provocative Church* is called 'Why doesn't the New Testament mention evangelism more often?' As he says, 'People like Peter, Paul and John preach wherever they go, found churches and evangelise like mad. But when they get around to writing they never seem to do what you'd expect them to do: urge church members to be active personal evangelists.' He answers his own question by saying:

> The task is to learn to live the Christian life before we talk about it: to develop a completely new way of living. And when that happens, the word of the evangelist, or the simple recounting of a personal journey to faith rings true because it connects with the reality experienced among God's people.[112]

Yet recent research suggests this may not be the norm in many churches. According to a survey of 2,859 respondents conducted in 2009 (82% of whom had been Christians for over ten years, and 67% in some type of church leadership role), 47% said they did not have a story to tell about how God has worked in their lives.[113] In another piece of research from the Evangelical Alliance, only 26% of people felt they had been well equipped to witness and share their faith with others.[114] The danger for church leaders is that often they think the problem is about competency. In other words, if they can equip their church members with ways to do evangelism then everything will be sorted. The reality is that for most people it's much more about a crisis in confidence in talking about their faith.

Michael Harvey has worked with many churches in developing a 'culture of invitation'.[115] He estimates that when he asks people in churches of all denominations if they can think of someone they could invite to a church event, around 70% say they can think of someone. But then when they are asked if they would actually invite that person, 85–95% say they would definitely not be inviting them. The reason is not the state of their local church, but simply their own lack of confidence in being able to invite someone or say anything about their faith. This is at heart an issue of discipleship.

Discipleship is not something that happens because of evangelism – that is, thinking it is only because we have held an Alpha Course or hosted a mission week that we need to consider discipleship. Evangelism is the consequence of discipleship. The 'Imagine' project, in their research about how the UK could be reached with the gospel, stated, 'The primary evangelistic problem that the Church faces is not the resistance of those who don't believe the good news about Jesus, but the failure to envision, equip and support those who do.'[116]

Part of my own wariness of the relationship between discipleship and evangelism has been caused by groups and churches I have met over the years who say things to me such as, 'We are presently concentrating on discipleship and fellowship and when we have sorted ourselves out and feel prepared and ready, we are going to get involved in evangelism.' But my experience has always been that they never do. They never seem to reach that tipping point of being ready to start communicating their faith in any form. I have come to realise that this is a faulty understanding of both discipleship and its relationship to evangelism. It is not a linear development, where you get yourself or your church sorted out and then start to look out beyond the church. It is much more a dynamic and synergistic development, where the elements combine to produce greater energy. In the New Testament evangelism is the overflow of authentic discipleship, but discipleship always happens in the context of intentional evangelism and mission. That is the context of the New Testament; it was so much part of the Christian life that it hardly needed to be mentioned. We need to understand and experience this powerful dynamic of discipleship and evangelism; they are two sides of the same coin.

Perhaps this is best illustrated in Jesus' famous words that we now call the great commission (Matthew 28:16–20). Jesus' final words to his disciples are not about how to be a good disciple but how to make new disciples. I was surprised a few years ago when I discovered the main verb of the sentence was not the command 'to go' but the imperative 'make disciples'. We make disciples *as we go*. So this is not about going to some far-distant land, but about living our normal lives in our streets, colleges and places of work, and allowing God to work with us and through us in his work of disciple-making. Chris Wright, in his major book *The Mission of God*, sums this up:

> The emphasis on the word Go in much mission rhetoric is undermined by the recognition that it is not an imperative at all in the text… Jesus did not primarily command his disciples to go: he commanded them to make disciples. But since he now commands them to make disciples of all nations, they will have to go… as a necessary condition of obeying the primary command.[117]

All the great talks I have heard (and some I have given) about the importance of 'going' did not really do justice to what Jesus was saying. Jesus' final words to his closest followers were saying, 'As I have discipled you over the last three years through my teaching, my actions, our shared experiences and living in close proximity to each other, now you do exactly the same with others as you live out your life every day. This is simply the process of the overflow of your own Christian life. You will also be teaching them to disciple others, and so the pattern continues throughout the ages.'

The concept of discipleship is very much on trend presently. Many conferences, magazine articles, talks, resources and social media conversations are around discipleship issues. But despite all this, I am not sure we know what discipleship actually is. It's worth noting that, like 'evangelism', 'discipleship' is not a word you find in the Bible (although, of course, the word 'disciple' is). The problem is that 'discipleship' can be used in such an all-encompassing way that it's difficult to pin down a precise definition. We often link it to specific actions, such as prayer or Bible reading, or to attending a particular course, as though doing certain things makes us disciples. This is certainly an aspect of discipleship, but it is bigger than that.

Willard provides a helpful definition of discipleship:

> A disciple is simply someone who decided to be with another person, under appropriate conditions, in order to become capable of doing what that person does or to become what that person is.[118]

Willard goes on to describe the heart of Christian discipleship: 'I need to be able to lead my life as Jesus would lead it if he were here.'[119] This means life is not simply about what I do, but is also about how I do it and who I am in doing it. Discipleship is not something we can drift into, although we can easily drift out of it, but it demands a deep intention to live this way in every aspect of our lives, empowered by the Spirit. It is how we respond to Jesus' call to 'follow me'. It requires a first-hand interaction with the risen Christ, who is present in our world today.

Disciples are people who are connected to and growing in God's love, but who are also connected in evangelism and mission as they live out that love in words and deeds. Discipleship is not about what we do with others when they 'make a decision' to follow Jesus; it is about what we are doing as God by his Spirit works in us, connecting us closely to the Father. Part of this has to involve being sent out to live in the world as his ambassadors and advocates in the same way that the Father sent the Son. The American researcher George Barna spent six years researching why and how people grow in their faith.

His work suggests that discipleship is not primarily related to church attendance, levels of giving, Bible knowledge or courses completed. 'It is about people through their relationships, experiences and knowledge aligning their intellect, emotions, behaviour and spirit with the calls and ways of God.'[120]

I was surprised to discover a few years ago that the word 'disciple' disappears from use in the New Testament after the gospels, with the exception of a few appearances in Acts. Why is this? Why do Peter and John, Jesus' disciples, not use the word at all in their letters? Surely this must be significant, but most contemporary writings on the subject totally ignore it.[121] Most of our recent discipleship theory and teachings are based on Jesus' interactions with the twelve disciples. Yet this ignores the rest of the New Testament, where the actual word 'disciple' is not used.

Most scholars suggest that for the New Testament writers the word 'disciple' was specifically associated with those who physically followed Jesus around. The rest of the New Testament, the epistles and Revelation, then has to deal with the question of how we can follow Jesus when he is not physically present. This is the situation that each of us faces daily.

What does this mean in practice for the formation of disciples who are therefore equipped to live in such a way that evangelism becomes a natural overflow of their relationship with Christ? I don't think there is one simple answer. I am sure that one course, however good, cannot provide everything that is required. We are talking about a lifetime of discipleship rather than a short-term burst for the beginning of the Christian life.

First, we need to enable and encourage disciples *to be hungry for God*. Discipleship should have the sense that 'what I have discovered is so good that I must have it and nothing else will or can do'. That kind of spiritual hunger is bound to overflow into evangelism. Yet, if we are honest, so much of our church life is humdrum, mundane, dull and drab. I meet many Christians who are simply bored by their own faith. I talk to a good number of experienced church leaders who confess to me that if they were not the leader they would not go to their church!

The job of church leaders, therefore, is not primarily to feed the flock, but to make them hungrier for God and present a vision of life with and in Christ. I remember clearly the conversation with one of my church leaders a few years ago. He had been a Christian for about 40 years and one day he came to tell me vigorously that he was not being fed presently by the church services and he was thinking of going to another church that would feed him. I found myself replying, 'Are you really telling me that you have been a Christian for most of your life, been involved in Christian leadership for 20 years and attended some great churches around the country, and despite all this you still cannot feed yourself?' I don't think this was the answer he was expecting! He looked totally stunned by my response, and a long conversation ensued. To be honest, I don't think he really understood what I was saying. His view of church was that it existed to nourish spiritual needs.

This conversation and my impromptu reply led me to spend much time pondering how we have created an organisation that can so easily provide people with information and knowledge about their faith but not get them to the point where they develop a vision for the whole of their life with Jesus and the hunger to make that become a reality for themselves and others. That does not mean there is no place for community and teaching; rather, it means these things are not ends in themselves, but some of the means by which this vision is worked out.

I worry that the way we exalt the church leader as 'expert in the faith' hampers this whole process of discipleship. People in our churches feel that they can never attain such expertise and then assume that they cannot live their life to the same level as the church leader. Yet proficiency in areas of specific knowledge that a church leader possesses is not the equivalent of being a disciple. If this were true, the Pharisees would have been commended for their discipleship! Discipleship is not about mere knowledge and actions; more importantly, it is about what I do with that knowledge and how I do what I do. It is about how the fruit of the Spirit – love, joy, peace, etc. (Galatians 5:22–26) – is growing amid our learning, working and living. Maybe leaders need to share not simply what they know and do, but also their own longings for God as they seek to live daily with Christ. How things might change as they share not only those longings of their heart but also the places where it is a struggle to live this out; where it might look good and active but maybe is lacking love, joy or peace. Might this be a start for developing church communities who are hungry for more of God in their lives?

Second, we need to understand that *disciples are discovering more and more of their true identity in Jesus*. In his writings, the apostle Paul doesn't ignore what it means to be a disciple of Jesus, even though he doesn't use the word itself. Often at the beginning of his letters he is fulsome in his encouragement to the church. This can easily be perceived as Paul buttering them up before he gets down to the real problems, but I think such encouragement lies at the heart of his discipleship training.

For example, when he writes to the church in Ephesus, he begins by reminding them who they really are. They are saints, faithful, blessed with every spiritual blessing, chosen to be holy and blameless, destined for adoption, redeemed through Jesus' blood and forgiven. They know God's will and plans, are obtaining an eternal inheritance and are receivers of the Holy Spirit (Ephesians 1:3–14). This is an awesome list. But what is Paul trying to do as he tells them who they are?

Paul is fundamentally changing the perspective of this very small group of followers of Jesus in a huge and prosperous city of 300,000 people. He is saying, 'This is who you are in Jesus; now become that person.' This is why he can write, 'You may know what is the hope to which he has called you, what are the riches of his glorious inheritance... and what is the immeasurable greatness of his power' (Ephesians 1:18–19).

They might feel like a small, beleaguered group of no-hopers, but there is another, grander, perspective. You are this person Paul describes, not because of skill, knowledge or hard work, but because of what Jesus has achieved through his death and resurrection for you. The discipleship challenge is now to become the person you are in Jesus. Paul encourages them 'to lead a life worthy of the calling to which you have been called' (Ephesians 4:1). He then goes on in the rest of his letter to demonstrate how this new identity is practically worked out in relationship with others, in pure living and in speaking the truth in love. This new identity changes who you are and the natural consequence of this is that it changes how you live your life.

Third, we need to be developing *disciples who are equipped for the whole of life* not just church life. The danger of using various courses or programmes as the basis of discipleship is that, however excellent their content, they end up becoming 'church socialisation' programmes; that is, they teach us how to behave and what to do in church, but they fail to equip us to fully live our lives in every aspect of our existence. As Mark Greene argues:

> In every culture and every land Jesus calls his followers to live out a radical set of values... Jesus calls us to live out this missionary adventure not just in the comparative safety of sanctuaries and homes but in workplaces, classrooms, hospitals, offices, factories, gyms... where the challenges to faith, the pressure on relationships and the difficulty of decision making are not only constant but often tense.[122]

Discipleship is not just about following Jesus at church or in a small group but following Jesus in the huge variety of places we find ourselves in. In the light of our new identity, this requires that our loves, fears, hopes and angers are reordered and rearranged by the gospel as we live it out in all parts of our life. I am not sure any one course or programme can deliver this (although I do think programmes have a role to play in this process); rather, it is about a number of important factors that combine together powerfully in discipleship.

Vision
We need to continually point people to what they are becoming in Jesus and say this is worth making reality, and it's worth more than anything else in the world. Willard provocatively comments, 'You call people to become disciples of Jesus by ravishing them with a vision of life in the Kingdom.'[123] You can't produce real vision by making people feel guilty or by sucking them into a ceaseless whirl of church activity. You must entice them into learning with Jesus and others to live the life God has given to us through Jesus. How might you create a vision for being these kinds of people in your church?

Transformation
It is worth thinking about where and how transformation happens. Discipleship is about a change in our identity that shapes our world view, and which therefore frames the temperament and practices of our lives. How can what we do or don't do support and encourage this?

Practice
Merely developing our knowledge of the Christian faith or acquiring more information is not enough; what matters is the way we live out our lives. It must impact not only our actions but also our attitudes. It will influence our life beyond church in our families, communities and wider society.

Context
Although God gives us basic principles about following Jesus, we will need to help people work these out in their own particular circumstances.

Intentional and accidental learning

Learning to do this cannot just happen through programmes and classes. Much of the learning happens in life as we reflect on our experiences and our reactions and responses in the light of Jesus. This is where we require two important things: *time* to reflect on what God is saying to us through our experiences and how he might be using these to change us and develop us; and *other people* who care for us and can help us in our reflections and responses.

That is why, fourth, we need *disciples who are willing to share the journey with others*. We cannot do this on our own. The church community is very much part of this process. It cannot be simply an individualistic pursuit. Jesus chose a group to be his disciples, and Paul wrote mostly to churches rather than individuals. For this journey, we need others to share life with. This often happens through an array of relationships and groups that are all part of our discipling process. There is no one single way, but what is important is that we choose to make ourselves accountable to some people and commit ourselves to invest in the lives of some others. My church small group is an important safe place for me. But also, for 25 years I have been part of a group of four people who meet four times a year with the express purpose of sharing our lives with and praying for each other.

Finally, we must be *disciples who are open to the opportunities* God may provide in our daily lives. We need to be alert to the people God may place before us and have the spiritual courage to respond to God's promptings. This seems to be behind Paul's words when he encourages the Christians at Colossae to devote themselves to prayer, to be alert and to make the most of their opportunities (Colossians 4:2–6). As we aim to live like Christ, we understand that we will find ourselves in situations that require us to explain our faith to people in appropriate ways. Evangelism is a natural overflow of our faith.

When our discipleship as individuals and churches involves these elements, evangelism will happen, and it will not be a forced or artificial practice. Disciples naturally become those who, as part of their discipleship, are witnessing to Jesus and his activity in their lives.

It's important to realise that the process of discipleship is not restricted to the church only. Many other forces and organisations are wanting to produce disciples, although they would not normally use this language. Graham Cray comments, 'If we are not part of a mutually discipling community the culture will disciple us.'[124] I was greatly helped in considering this by James Smith's *Desiring the Kingdom*.[125] Smith helped me to see how entering a shopping centre is a discipling experience and education. In every shop we enter, displays, information and advertising fuel our imagination with the promise of what we might be – our true self – as we drive a particular car or use a certain shampoo. In much advertising, we are told very little about the product; instead, we are clearly shown who we become as we have or use the product – popular, beautiful, glamorous, sexy, successful and so on. We get glimpses of this new life as we are shown images of celebrities with the product. They are the vision of what we might become. They embody for us what the lifestyle, or discipleship, might look like, so we can begin to imagine ourselves in the same situation, that we too might imitate them and become like them. Lastly, we are told that to become true disciples, there are disciplines that we need to submit to, anything from a certain cosmetic regime to a diet that gives us a celebrity-style body. The promise is that these disciplines will enable us to find joy, peace, fulfilment and flourishing as we become the real us!

Advertisers have discovered one key ingredient of discipleship. They understand that it is primarily not about facts, information or training but our hearts and desires. The issue is not what we know but what or who we love. This is what really defines us as human beings. We are driven much more by our heart, as we respond to the promise of who we might be, our true identity, and this is why vision is so important.

I wonder if the two key questions we need to ask about our discipleship and evangelism are those suggested by Willard in *Knowing Christ Today*.[126] First, he suggests, we need to ask what kind of people we are called to be. What does it mean to be truly human, made in God's image? Who are we created to be in Jesus Christ? In the light of this information, we then need to ask, second, what kind of community is able to raise people like this. I have often thought that, if I were planting a church from scratch again, these would be the two questions I would start with. They would continually keep before us the close connection between evangelism and discipleship for our own development, but also for the life of the church and for the lives of those God has put around us.

Questions

- How would you describe the relationship between evangelism and discipleship?

- How do you ensure that discipleship does not become inward-looking and church-focused?

- How would you measure discipleship in your congregation?

- Can you identify ways in which our culture is discipling us as leaders and members of churches? How does it do this?

10

Note to self: 'Why am I doing this?'

David Male

There are two major questions to consider as we think about our motivation for evangelism. Firstly, do we truly believe that the living God is active in his creation? By 'believe', I don't mean whether or not we understand intellectually or can give the statement our mental assent. I mean: do we really live and act as if God is at work? Is that our primary assumption in all that we do? Much of what the media tells us every day would suggest that God is either absent or inactive. If there is a God, which is unlikely, he is at best a distant deity whose role has been superseded by science and reason. But if we really believe that he is still in business and is constantly active in his world, we must ask, secondly, could he possibly use me in his activity? Is it possible or likely that God would want to use me, with all my limitations, in his work? These are profound questions and our answers to them will shape our evangelism and, indeed, our lives.

It is these two questions that Jesus is answering as he arrives in Galilee proclaiming the good news and saying, 'The time is fulfilled, and the kingdom of God has come near; repent, and believe in the good news' (Mark 1:15). Jesus was announcing that this was the key moment in history, the fulfilment of all that Israel had been waiting for. God had come to his people in the person of Jesus, and this pivotal moment required a definite response from his listeners. The word translated 'repent' is not simply about saying sorry to God or others; it presents the idea of a decisive break, a radical cutting loose from old ties and affiliations that hold us back from following God wholeheartedly. To believe the good news is to take Jesus completely at his word, to follow and obey him, wherever it takes us and whatever it involves.

The good news for us is that, through Jesus, the door to the future is wide open and we are called to walk through it in faith. Immediately after Jesus' dramatic announcement, he put his teaching into action as he called the first disciples to 'fish for people' (Mark 1:17). Would they trust that God was at work in their locality in Galilee and that he wanted to use a bunch of fishermen? As Jesus said, 'Follow me', would they take him at his word and follow? Like the first disciples, we must decide whether we will take Jesus at his word and cooperate with him in this adventure of being fishers of people.

As long as evangelism is viewed today as arrogant, hectoring or simply intolerant, it can be easier to keep our faith to ourselves. So it is worth considering what might enable us to reconnect with God, with his message of good news and with people outside the church. As already mentioned, one of the major problems we face is the belief that evangelism is for the professionals – missionaries or church leaders, those who are supremely gifted in this area or those with specific training in evangelism – and that amateurs should keep out of the way. But I believe it's for everyone, because it's not about training, knowledge or qualifications. It's about being ourselves and trusting that God can use us.

What you read in this chapter will probably not be new to you, but I want it to act as a reminder of why you are – or can be – involved in evangelism. I hope that by the end you will be thinking, 'I can do this with God's help.'

It's not what we know, it's

At the most basic level, evangelism
It's not a technique, it's not a trans
slick presentation. Evangelism come
and is accomplished by God. It is
engineer – yet we should not be pas...
God, by his Spirit, is at work today and calls us to wo...
his world, enabling people to encounter him and seeing lives and
communities transformed.

Sometimes I attend prayer meetings that feel as if we are trying to
persuade God to act, as if we are begging a reluctant God to rouse
himself. I remember being involved with a mission at a college in
Cheltenham, where I had organised a question-and-answer session
to which over 20 students had come along. One bright young
woman asked many probing questions about faith, God and the
Bible, so when I returned to the college the following week and
discovered that one of the people at the session had decided to
become a follower of Jesus, I was sure it would be the woman with
all the questions. I was astonished to discover that it was not her but
another woman who had not said a word. I could not even remember
her being there. Through our techniques and expectations, we can
often limit our expectations of what God can do.

When we look at ourselves and our church, we might wonder what
we can achieve, because of our own smallness and the enormity
of the task. But we should be looking at God, who is active in his
world as he always has been and always will be. The real question
is whether we will take him at his word and join in with what he is
doing. John V. Taylor begins his classic book on mission by reminding
us that 'the chief actor in the historic mission of the Christian church
is the Holy Spirit. He is the director of the whole enterprise. The
mission consists of the things he is doing in the world.'[127]

like learning to swim. When you learn to swim, teachers
what you need to do (as well as giving you important
rances about why you will float and not sink). You can use
ts and armbands to help you to practise until you are ready to
wim unaided. But one day, however well you know the theory and
however much you have practised with floats, you have to trust the
water and lift your feet off the bottom of the pool. In evangelism,
there will be many times when your faith is stretched – when you
will have to take Jesus at his word, lift your feet off the bottom of the
pool and trust that he will support you.

It's not what we know, it's the love we experience

The simple truth is that we are much more likely to express love if
we first experience it – and we know this in all aspects of our human
relationships. For example, we recognise the importance of having a
loving, secure home for the development of children and their ability
to love and relate to others. Evangelism has been helpfully defined as
the natural overflow of our own encounter with Jesus. We are trying
to express to people, in words and actions, what a relationship with
the loving God looks like, but at the heart of this description is our
own present experience of this reality. As John V. Taylor comments,
'In all true evangelism the church is talking to itself, if it did but
know.'[128]

In linking our present experience of God with our evangelism, there
are two important issues. First, we need to ensure that the order is
correct. God does not love us more because we express our faith to
others. We are not doing it to get good marks from God in some kind
of cosmic test. We communicate our faith because we know his love
and it is transforming us. Second, if our present experience of God is
as someone who is distant to us, a burdensome deity whom we must
continually please or placate, or a kill-joy who is out to make life
miserable for us, why would we inflict such a God on anyone else?

Some of the most amazing words in the gospels are the Father's words to Jesus at his baptism: 'You are my Son, the Beloved; with you I am well pleased' (Mark 1:11). It is worth noting that this affirmation came before Jesus' public ministry had begun, before his proclamation of the good news or his calling of the disciples. The Father was not 'well pleased' with Jesus because of his achievements. He was pleased because of who Jesus *was* – because of their relationship. Although that was a unique relationship, I think the words apply to us. Take time to hear God speaking to you: 'You are my daughter/son; I love you and delight in you.' I suspect that even as we read, many of us struggle to grasp the enormity of God's love for us. Maybe there are voices inside us that want to add the word 'but' to this sentence of affirmation from God: '… but you could do better'; '… but I am a bit disappointed in your recent behaviour'; '… but you could pray more'; '… but you could be more like…'. Yet such criticisms never come from God's side.

This is grace in action, and these are words that send us out. We are loved not because of our accomplishments, achievements or accolades, but because God is loving and loves us. If we could really grasp it at the depth of our being, we would be unable to stay quiet. This is why Paul prays for the church in Ephesus, 'I pray that you may have the power to comprehend… what is the breadth and length and height and depth, and to know the love of Christ that surpasses knowledge, so that you may be filled with all the fullness of God' (Ephesians 3:18–19). If we knew how much we were loved, nothing would hold us back. It would help us to recognise that the secret of our lives is not at the circumference, with all its endless activities, but right at the centre, with the love we experience from God. The evangelist Leighton Ford writes, 'Each of us is called to a life… not shaped by inner compulsions, or captive to outer expectations, but drawn by the inner voice of love. But I do realise that this requires not so much doing for God as paying attention to what God is doing.'[129]

It's not what you know, it's who you know

A good question to ask yourself is, 'Who has God put around me? Who am I with in my daily life?' These people are not there by accident. If you think about your family, your colleagues, your neighbours or your social contacts, you will already have a good list of people. I wonder how often you ask yourself what God thinks about them. They all really matter to God, not as targets for his gospel but as men, women and children created and loved by him. Do you see the people around you as God sees them? As I was writing this chapter, someone who is not a Christian and works in the college where I am based told me that his mum had died suddenly at the weekend. How does God feel for that person today and what impact does that have on my response to him? I was able to talk with him and then asked if I could pray for him. We prayed together in our little college kitchen.

You never know how and where God might be at work and how he might want to use you in that work. A couple of years ago, I went with my son's football team to a tournament in Bournemouth. We stayed in caravans and a number of other parents went as well. To tell the truth, I did not want to go, so I tried to persuade my wife to go without me. April is not a great time to stay in a caravan, and I was tired and just wanted to stay at home and relax. After the matches, there was a lot of time to socialise, and we ended up talking with two other couples on different occasions. Over a drink, one parent suddenly said that she knew lots about other faiths but hardly anything about Christianity. Could we tell her more about the Christian faith? Another parent confessed how scared she was of dying.

These discussions showed me clearly that we must be alert to God's activity and close enough to people to be present when needed. Conversations have continued with these two couples and they have both attended church events with us. I'm also reminded of the importance of praying that God would make us aware of his activity among others: to be honest, though, I had not prayed much about that football trip.

I remember one particular conversation with a stranger in the steam room at the local gym. I had just finished a workout and was looking forward to a bit of relaxation. As soon as I walked into the room, a man who was already there started talking to me. Although I did not want to chat, he started telling me about his business producing vinyl records, which was extremely successful. I knew what the next question was going to be: 'And what do you do?' I had no choice but to explain that I was a vicar who was trying to create a church for people who do not go to church. He said to me, 'I have been so successful and made lots of money but I've realised that there must be more to life than this. I have got to the top but it's not satisfying me.'

I have never known a stranger to be so honest with me. Fortunately no one else joined us in the steam room and we talked for about 20 minutes about what life is really about. By the time we had finished, I was nearly passing out with the heat, but I did not want to end the discussion prematurely. I was struck especially by his words at the end of our time. He said, 'Thanks for talking to me. I have been looking for so long to talk about this with someone, but none of my friends wanted to.' It made me think about how many thousands of people are out there with questions that God is raising in them, yet they have no one to talk to about them. What can we do to be available to God and to people around us?

How much we reflect God's priority for people will show up in the way we use our time. I wonder what your diary says about you and the importance of those whom God has placed around you? Are you making them a priority and developing genuine relationships? Or are you so busy that you never have the time or mental space to connect in the way God wants you to?

It's not what you know, it's why you are here now

I am writing this book today because, 40 years ago, some young people, most of whom were at university, gave up part of their summer holidays and came to my town to organise a beach mission. A schoolfriend of mine, who was not involved in any church, heard about it and invited me along. I was attracted initially by the sports activities, and then, as time went by, I was profoundly impressed by the leaders. At first I didn't go to any of the 'religious bits', just the sports in the afternoons. In the second week, though, I started to attend the talks and Bible studies in the mornings. For the first time in my life, I heard the good news of Jesus explained in a way that made sense to a young person. Three months later, after thinking deeply about what I had heard, I knelt one night by my bed and asked Jesus to take over my life. Those same people helped me to grow in my faith over the next ten years, gave me my first experiences of leadership and equipped me to view evangelism as a very natural activity that every Christian could do.

I sometimes wonder what would have happened if those people had not bothered to come to my town. What if they had decided to use their summer holidays for a quiet break or a holiday, or had not written me letters over the next ten years encouraging me in my faith and teaching me about prayer and Bible reading? The simple answer is that I do not know, but the memory has always motivated me in thinking about how I might be used by God. I want to give others the opportunity I was given to meet Jesus and be transformed by him.

It is important that we regularly reconnect with our own story of how we came to faith. It reminds us of what God has done for us, and the vital role that others have played in living and communicating the gospel to us. We too often think of it as being simply in the past, but to reconnect with the way God was at work reminds us that he is the same God, and is at work today in similar ways, if we have eyes to see it.

It's not what you know, it's who you are

One of the dangers when thinking about evangelism is our instinctive sense that it's 'just not me'. Perhaps we don't fit the classic 'stereotypes' for evangelism in personality, training or outlook. Sometimes the people who lead evangelism training share lots of exciting stories about how God has used them almost every day to lead somebody to faith in Christ. We can easily think that if we were like 'so-and-so' we would be able to get involved like that as well. Yet I am convinced that God wants to use us as we are and not as we think we should be. God wants to work through *our* character, background, personality and interests. He loves us as we are, in the way he has made us; and he wants to use us like that. We don't have to become someone else or a caricature of ourselves before we can be involved in God's adventure in evangelism.

I will always remember a woman in her 70s whom I met in Huddersfield, called Mary Moorhouse. When I arrived to work with a church to help them with their evangelism, I spent time with many people who had discovered Jesus through the church. I wanted to learn more about why and how they had found faith in Jesus. As they told me their stories, I realised that most of them began with the words, 'Well, one day I met this lady, Mary Moorhouse.' Countless people put the beginning of their spiritual journey down to a chance meeting with Mary. Mary is not famous in Christian circles but is one of the most effective witnesses I have ever met.

I was eager to find out what her evangelistic method was – it had to be amazing. But on meeting her I discovered that her method would probably not be included in any handbook on evangelism. Like thousands of other church members across the country, Mary took the parish newsletter round to the houses near where she lived. Through this seemingly mundane activity, she met lots of people who did not go to church but were walking their dogs, gardening, unpacking their cars and so on. She would stop and talk with them, and through this she often discovered newcomers to the area who didn't know many people yet, or she met people facing difficult circumstances who wanted someone to talk with. From these humble beginnings, through her weekly delivery of the newsletter, she began to develop relationships. She would gently talk about the church she attended and her own faith in Jesus. Over time, many people with whom she had struck up conversations began to do things like having their children baptised, attending church, getting to know Christians, joining church groups and eventually developing a vibrant faith. Some went on to become key leaders in the church.

When I talked to Mary about all this amazing work, she was flabbergasted by my assertion that she might be a brilliant witness. She told me that she felt she had no gifts in this area but simply gave out newsletters and loved getting to know those who lived in her area. That sounds like being an excellent witness to me! She was a friendly neighbour who – armed with a parish magazine, a smile and a cheery word – was greatly used by God because she had found her own way of obeying and following her Lord.

God can use Mary, and he can use any of us. We do not have to fit into some predetermined mould to be involved in the adventure of evangelism. The Chinese Christian leader Brother Yun summed this up when he wrote, 'It's not the greatest people who change the world but weak people in the hands of a great God.'[130] The apostle Paul, talking about his own ministry, wrote these words, given him by Christ: 'My grace is sufficient for you, for power is made perfect in weakness' (2 Corinthians 12:9). Do we really believe this? God can use us as we are.

It's not what you know, it's who you are with

Evangelism is a team game. We tend to think of it as an individual endeavour but it is related to being part of the Christian community, the church. When I was a new Christian, I received the subliminal message that Jesus is great but we're sorry about the church that comes with him. Yet the New Testament's message is that church, this new community, is wonderful and is to be viewed as a signpost to and foretaste of heaven.

For many people, the first gospel they encounter is what they see happening at their local church – not just the services and activities but the attitudes and priorities of those who attend the church and the warmth of the relationships to be found there. This will have a significant impact on whether they stick around to find out more about Jesus.

The questions we need to ask, therefore, are 'What is our role in the team?' and 'What does our Christian community say about the good news?' Evangelism cannot be dissociated from the life of the local church.

It's not what you know, it's where you are

The coming of Jesus, the Son of God, in a particular time and place reminds us that 'place' matters to God. He is the God of the universe but he is also the God of the particular. It is important to consider how much we value our immediate surroundings. We are not there by accident. It can be easy to wish we were somewhere else, or feel that our current situation is a staging-post on the way to the place we are really trying to get to. Yet God loves the place where we are, and calls us to begin to see it in the same way.

When I lived in Huddersfield, I used to climb a local landmark called Castle Hill, from which I could look out over the entire town centre. It helped me to get a perspective on the way God saw the town and his amazing love for its inhabitants. It reminded me that the vast majority had no contact with any church, and many of them were living without a life-transforming relationship with Jesus.

Where we live matters to God. It may not be the location we would have chosen, or the place where we thought we might be, but we are not there by mistake. God is active and calls us to work with him in that place.

So will you take Jesus at his word and follow him in this amazing work of evangelism? Take note of his reassurance that he can and will use you exactly as you are, as you trust yourself to him.

Questions

- What are *your* main motivations for evangelism?

In the light of reading this book:

- Write down three actions you are going to take as a church in response to reading this book.

- Identify training and teaching needs that this book has helped to focus.

- How, as as a leader, will you model evangelism in the future?

Further resources

Here are some resources for evangelism that we have found useful:

Books on evangelism

William Abraham, *The Logic of Evangelism* (Hodder, 1989) – Classic exploration of the link between evangelism and discipleship.

Steve Addison, *Pioneering Movements: Leadership that multiplies disciples and churches* (IVP, 2016) – Looks at what kind of leadership is required for mission.

Francis Adeney, *Graceful Evangelism: Christian witness in a complex world* (Baker Academic, 2010) – A comprehensive treatment of evangelism, from biblical models to contemporary practice.

Mike Booker and Mark Ireland, *Making New Disciples: Exploring the paradoxes of evangelism* (SPCK Publishing, 2015) – A very helpful evaluation of evangelism resources.

Walter Brueggemann, *Biblical Perspectives on Evangelism: Living in a three-storied universe* (Abingdon Press, 1993) – A stimulating biblical and theological exploration of the meaning of evangelism.

Sam Chan, *Evangelism in a Skeptical World* (Zondervan, 2018) – Some really good theological and practical thinking about evangelism in a postmodern world.

Tim Chester and Steve Timmis, *Everyday Church* (IVP, 2011) – An excellent book on creating attractive missional communities.

Stephen Cottrell, *From the Abundance of the Heart: Catholic evangelism for all Christians* (Darton, Longman and Todd, 2006) – Looks at practical ways of developing structures and ministries that establish a culture of evangelism in the local church.

Jim Currin, *Sharing Faith the Jesus Way* (BRF, 2011) – Examines how Jesus shared the good news.

Don Everts and Doug Shaupp, *Pathways to Jesus* (IVP, 2009) – Research on how people come to faith today.

John Finney, *Emerging Evangelism* (Darton, Longman and Todd, 2004) – Stimulating discussion on contemporary evangelism.

Pope Francis, *Evangelii Gaudium: The joy of the gospel* (Libreria Editrice Vaticana, 2013) – A powerful exhortation on the need for God's love to fill our lives and witness in today's world.

Michael Frost, *Surprise the World: The five habits of highly missional people* (Navpress,2015) – Great practical suggestions for talking about faith.

Randy Newman, *Questioning Evangelism: Engaging people's hearts the way Jesus did*, second edition (Kregel Publications, 2018) – Looks at how using dialogue in evangelism can give people confidence in talking about faith.

Rebecca Manley Pippert, *Out of the Saltshaker*, revised edition (IVP, 2010) – In our opinion, still one of the best books on personal evangelism.

Rick Richardson, *Reimagining Evangelism: Inviting friends on a spiritual journey* (Scripture Union, 2007) – Takes a fresh look at what personal evangelism could be.

Alan Roxburgh and Martin Robinson, *Practices for the Refounding of God's People: The missional challenge of the west* (Church Publishing Inc, 2018) – A deep engagement with the ways the gospel transforms society.

Laurence Singlehurst, *Sowing, Reaping, Keeping: People-sensitive evangelism* (IVP, 2006) – An excellent book on the process of evangelism for individuals and churches.

Bryan Stone, *Evangelism after Christendom: The theology and practice of Christian witness* (Brazos Press, 2010) – An in-depth treatment of evangelism from a Wesleyan perspective.

Bryan Stone, *Evangelism after Pluralism* (Baker Academic 2018) – Looks at what it means to evangelise ethically in a multicultural climate.

Rico Tice, *Honest Evangelism: How to talk about Jesus when it's tough* (The Good Book Company, 2015) – Practical help to articulate your faith.

Robert Warren, *Developing Healthy Churches* (CHP, 2012) – Great practical advice on how to revitalise and develop existing churches.

Chris Wright, *The Mission of God: Unlocking the Bible's grand narrative* (IVP, 2006) – An important book that argues convincingly that the entire Bible is generated by and is all about God's mission.

Chris Wright, *The Mission of God's People: A biblical theology of the church's mission* (Zondervan, 2010) – A follow-on to his 2006 book above, asking the 'so what' questions for the people of God in each new generation.

'The Grove Evangelism Series' – concise booklets exploring key areas in evangelism. See **grovebooks.co.uk/collections/evangelism**.

See also lots of resources for evangelism at **greatcommission.co.uk/about**.

Evangelism training courses for the church

Beautiful Lives (ReSource Publications) – a course to encourage people to share their faith with friends and neighbours. **disciplekit.org/resource/beautiful-lives-sharing-our-faith-with-friends-and-neighbours**

Blowing Your Cover – a course designed to equip and release Christians to share their faith confidently and impact their community in a way that best fits their character and personality. **blowingyourcover.com**

Faith Pictures (Church Army) – a short course designed to help Christians talk naturally to friends, neighbours and colleagues about what they believe. The heart of the course is about helping people to identify a single picture or image that embodies something of their faith. **churcharmy.org/Groups/266913/Church_Army/ms/Faith_Pictures/Faith_Pictures.aspx**

Fruitfulness on the Frontline (LICC) – a suite of resources offering a fresh, simple framework for discovering a rich variety of ways God may work in us and through us right where we are. **licc.org.uk/resources/discover-fruitfulness-on-the-frontline**

Journey to Faith (Arthur Rank Centre) – a simple two-session course to envision and equip a local rural church. **germinate.net/mission/journey-to-faith**

Just Walk across the Room (Willow Creek Association) – a four-week course encouraging people to go beyond their circle of comfort. **willowcreek.org.uk/product/just-walk-across-the-room-all**

Living and Telling (Agape) – a practical course on sharing faith. **shop.agape.org.uk/livingandtelling.html**

Mission Academy Live (Hope) – a series of ten innovative video-based sessions, each one empowering young people as missional disciples within a small-group context. **hopetogether.org.uk/Groups/290576/Mission_Academy_Live.aspx**

Natural Evangelism Course (J. John) – a six-session course, which provides a simple, yet insightful training programme for all churches wanting to encourage and equip their members towards more effective friendship evangelism. **canonjjohn.com/the-natural-evangelism-course**

Stepping into Evangelism (Church Army) – practical advice, tips and exercises to help you and your church reach out to others in words and action. **churcharmy.org.uk/Groups/291072/Church_Army/web/What_we_do/Resources/Stepping_into_evangelism/Stepping_into_evangelism.aspx**

Talking Jesus (Hope) – six encouraging, video-based sessions with short films, inspirational, short testimonies, real-life examples from people who are talking Jesus, and a short, easy-to-follow course book. **talkingjesus.org**

Talking of God (Methodist Church) – a free four-session course to help people tell their own Christian story. **methodist.org.uk/our-work/learning/discipleship/journeying-with-others/small-groups/resourcing-your-small-group/talking-of-god**

Evangelism resources to use with those outside the church

The first four resources on this list come from the Ugly Duckling Company, which exists to stimulate conversations about 'the big questions' of life for people who are spiritual seekers but would not come to a church service or even an evangelistic event. Find out more about all these courses at **theuglyducklingcompany.com**.

Puzzling Questions – a six-week course which explores six of the most popular questions asked by those who are interested in spirituality but are outside the life of the local church.

Table Talk – a resource to encourage natural conversations around spiritual issues. **table-talk.org**

The Happiness Lab – a six-week experiment that enables delegates to explore what psychologists, doctors and faith leaders say will make people happier.

Resolve – a four-week course designed to help you make lifelong positive changes. Each week, participants explore what the experts have to say, talk to others in the group about what they think and engage in a variety of practical exercises to help them accomplish their goals.

Life Explored (Christianity Explored Ministries) – an exciting new way to share the gospel in today's highly visual culture. It's designed to speak powerfully to those who don't consider themselves to be religious and have never read the Bible. The seven interactive sessions are based on stunning videos shot all over the globe. **ceministries.org/Articles/467668/Courses/Life_Explored/ Factsheet.aspx**

Soularium (Agape) – a survey tool based on images designed to initiate spiritual conversations with non-believers. **shop.agape.org. uk/soularium.html**

Why on Earth? (Church Army and SPCK) – sessions that open up some of life's hardest questions in an accessible way. Each session offers simple first steps in exploring a difficult subject. It does not aim to give final answers, just starting-points. **whyonearth.me/ Groups/307483/Home.aspx**

The Y Course – this eight-week course helps people face life's biggest questions and introduces them to Jesus. **ycourse.com**

Notes

1 George Barna, *Evangelism That Works* (Regal Books, 1995), p. 22.
2 John Finney, *Emerging Evangelism* (DLT, 2004), gives a helpful historical perspective in chapters 4 and 5.
3 C.H. Hopkins, *John R. Mott, A Biography* (Eerdmans, 1979), p. 342.
4 Philip Jenkins, *The Next Christendom* (OUP, 2007), p. 2.
5 *Towards the Conversion of England* (The Press and Publications Board of the Church Assembly, 1945).
6 *Towards the Conversion of England*, p. 1.
7 *Towards the Conversion of England*, p. 2.
8 *Towards the Conversion of England*, p. 3.
9 *Towards the Conversion of England*, p. 122.
10 *Towards the Conversion of England*, p. 49.
11 See **licc.org.uk/imagine**.
12 *Towards the Conversion of England*, p. ix.
13 *Towards the Conversion of England*, p. 147.
14 **liccimagine.blogspot.co.uk/2010/06/evangelisation-of-uk-liccimagine.html#more**
15 George Barna, *Evangelism that Works* (Regal Books, 1995), p. 16.
16 John Finney, *Finding Faith Today* (Bible Society, 1992), p. 25.
17 Mike Booker and Mark Ireland, *Evangelism: Which way now?* 2nd edn (CHP, 2005), p. 66.
18 **uk-england.alpha.org**
19 Finney, *Emerging Evangelism*, pp. 82–85.
20 For more details about the church, see David Male, *Church Unplugged* (Authentic, 2008).
21 Stephen Hunt, *The Alpha Enterprise* (Ashgate, 2004), p. 195.
22 Finney, *Emerging Evangelism*, p. 86.
23 Finney, *Emerging Evangelism*, p. 87.
24 Booker and Ireland, *Evangelism*, p. 48.
25 For more information see **table-talk.org**.
26 Jon Cook, 'Five things you didn't know about Stormzy', *TimeOut*, 13 April 2015, **timeout.com/london/music/five-things-you-didnt-know-about-stormzy**.

27 John Stackhouse, *Evangelical Landscapes* (Baker Academic, 2002), p. 163.

28 For more information see **streetpastors.co.uk**.

29 For more information see **uk.24-7prayer.com**.

30 For more information see **duffett.wordpress.com**.

31 For more information see **inspiremovement.org**.

32 Os Guinness, *The Gravedigger File* (Hodder, 1983), p. 51 (italics original).

33 Steve Bruce, *Religion in Modern Britain* (Oxford University Press, 1995), p. 37.

34 The report can be found at **news.bbc.co.uk/1/shared/bsp/hi/ pdfs/03_04_07_tearfundchurch.pdf**.

35 *All God's Children? Children's Evangelism in Crisis* (Church House Publishing, 1991).

36 *All God's Children*, pp. 3–4.

37 Peter Brierley, *The Tide Is Running Out* (Christian Research, 2000).

38 Max Planck, *A Scientific Autobiography* (Williams & Norgate, 1950), p. 155.

39 Quoted in John Coffey, 'Secularisation: is it inevitable?' *Cambridge Papers*, 2001.

40 Quoted in Rodney Stark, 'Secularisation, R.I.P', *Sociology of Religion*, 60, 1999, p. 249.

41 'The desecularisation of the world: a global overview', in P. Berger (ed.) *The Desecularisation of the World: Resurgent Religion and World Politics* (Eerdmans, 1999), p. 2.

42 Grace Davie, *Religion in Britain since 1945* (Blackwell, 1994), p. 107. The second edition of this book now has a different subtitle: *Religion in Britain: A persistent paradox* (Wiley Blackwell, 2015).

43 Richard Middleton and Brian Walsh, *Truth is Stranger Than It Used To Be* (IVP, 1995), p. 43.

44 *The Observer*, November 1993.

45 Lesslie Newbigin, *The Gospel in a Pluralist Society* (SPCK, 1989), p. 220.

46 John Drane, *Evangelism for a New Age* (Marshall, 1994), p. 17.

47 Jean-François Lyotard, *The Postmodern Condition: A report on knowledge* (Manchester University Press, 1984), p. xxiv.

48 Terry Eagleton, *The Illusions of Postmodernity* (Blackwell, 1996), p. vii.

49 Peter Berger, *The Heretical Imperative: Contemporary possibilities of religious affirmation* (Collins, 1980).

50 Berger, *Heretical Imperative*, p 62.

51   Rudolf Bultmann, 'New Testament and mythology', in H. Bartsch (ed.), *Kerygma and Myth* (SPCK, 1953), p. 5.

52   Berger, *Heretical Imperative*, pp. 62–63.

53   Berger, *Heretical Imperative*, p. 186.

54   Berger, *Heretical Imperative*, p. 61.

55   See, for example, Peter's experience at the house of Cornelius in Acts 10, or Paul's experience in following the Spirit's lead in Acts 13:2 or 16:10.

56   Roland Allen, *The Spontaneous Expansion of the Church* (Eerdmans, 1962, originally published 1927), p. 6.

57   Quoted from his pamphlet *Evangelism: Some principles and experiments* (1936) in Owen Brandon, *Battle for the Soul* (Hodder, 1960), p. 46.

58   'The biblical basis of evangelism', in John Stott, *Let the Earth Hear His Voice* (Lausanne Papers, 1974), p. 68–69.

59   Published respectively by The Navigators, Campus Crusade for Christ (now 'Agape'), and St Matthias Press.

60   For example, C.H. Dodd's *The Apostolic Preaching and Its Developments* (Hodder & Stoughton, 1936).

61   A good example of this is to be found in the summary material in John's gospel, after Jesus' interview with Nicodemus (John 3:16–19), which is sometimes attributed to Jesus himself but seems more likely to have been composed by the gospel writer.

62   Compare, for example, Paul's sermon in Athens (Acts 17) with Peter's at Pentecost (Acts 2). Both are significant in specifically addressing questions raised by the hearers (Acts 2:6–7, 12–13; Acts 17:22–23). As a result of differing contexts (one conversant with the Old Testament, the other with dominant forms of Greek philosophy), the two sermons take differing shapes.

63   *Evangelism Today: Good news or bone of contention?* (Christian Journals, 1976), pp. 80, 82.

64   *Evangelism Today*, p. 81.

65   See, for example, Luke 10:36 for an example of the former, and Mark 10:17–18 for the latter.

66   See Acts 2:36; 3:20; 4:26; 5:31; 10:36, 42; 13:23, 38–39; 17:31.

67   Other approaches to this question might use Jesus' conversation with the rich ruler about what real goodness is (Mark 10:17–27 and parallels). The sincerity question could be addressed through passages such as Matthew 7:21–23; 10:33 or John 14:6, where Jesus speaks about his exclusive and determinative role in relation to

God. Consider also the stories of the two gates and the two builders (Matthew 7:3–14; 7:24–27).

68 For example, Matthew 6:19–21; 19:23 (Mark 10:21–23; Luke 18:22–25); Luke 6:20, 24; 12:15, 16–21; 16:13, 19–31.

69 Matthew 20:26–28 (Mark 10:43–45); Mark 7:20–23; 12:38–40; Luke 9:46–48; 18:10–14.

70 For example, Matthew 5:38–39; Mark 3:27; 7:20–23; John 12:31–32.

71 The Greek word for 'repentance' (*metanoia*) literally means an 'after mind'.

72 Alasdair MacIntyre, *After Virtue: A study in moral theory* (Bloomsbury, 3rd ed. 2007), p. 246.

73 It is striking in this context that Jesus often starts his dialogues with a comment and proceeds to tell a story to illustrate it (for example, Luke 12:15 leading to vv. 16–21).

74 Peter's speech is effectively an exposition of three Old Testament texts (Joel 2 and Psalms 16 and 110).

75 John Reader, *Beyond All Reason: The limits of post-modern theology* (Aureus, 1997), p. 84.

76 Compare 1 Corinthians 1:18–25; 2:14; 3:19.

77 Walter Brueggemann, *Re-describing Reality* (Fortress, 1997), p. xx.

78 Walter Brueggemann, *Biblical Perspectives on Evangelism* (Abingdon Press, 2001), p. 129.

79 Trevor Hart, *Faith Thinking: The dynamics of Christian theology* (SPCK, 1995), p. 153.

80 Alasdair MacIntyre, *Three Rival Versions of Moral Enquiry* (University of Notre Dame Press, 1990), p. 125.

81 Quoted in Vincent Donovan, *Christianity Rediscovered* (SCM, 1982), p. vii.

82 See, for example, his words to the disciples in John 13:35 in the context of chapters 13—17.

83 *The Truth Shall Make You Free: The Lambeth Conference 1988 – The Reports, Resolutions and Pastoral Letters from the Bishops* (Anglican Consultative Council, 1988), p. 29.

84 *The Truth Shall Make You Free*, p. 32.

85 David Bosch, *Transforming Mission: Paradigm shifts in theology of mission* (Orbis, 2nd ed., 2011), p. 459.

86 Lesslie Newbigin, *Honest Religion for Secular Man* (SCM, 1966), pp. 101–02.

87 The gospel of Matthew appears to have been written in a situation in which the Christian community is working out its relationship to

the synagogue, while Peter's first epistle was written to 'diaspora' believers who were working out their corporate identity in the wider Roman Empire.

88 Acts 13:45, 50; 14:2, 19; 18:12.
89 The idea of 'home' is used in the gospels (see, for example, Mark 2:1), but Jesus and the disciples rarely seem to have been there. More characteristically, Jesus talks of having 'nowhere to lay his head' (Matthew 8:20).
90 There are other verbal parallels with Ezekiel 34 as well.
91 Donovan, *Christianity Rediscovered*, pp. 15–16.
92 Donovan, *Christianity Rediscovered*, p. 101.
93 Quoted in Donovan, *Christianity Rediscovered*, p. vii.
94 Donovan, *Christianity Rediscovered*, p. vii.
95 Jürgen Moltmann, *The Church in the Power of the Spirit* (SCM, 1977), p. 10.
96 Sylvia Collins-Mayo, *The Faith of Generation Y* (CHP, 2010).
97 Stephen Bevans and Roger Schroeder, *Prophetic Dialogue* (Orbis Books, 2009), p. 1.
98 John V. Taylor, *The Go-Between God* (SCM, 1972), p. 53.
99 'What the Leaders Said' (LICC, 2004).
100 'Apprentice', 2009. **yumpu.com/en/document/view/37723596/ apprentice-the-london-institute-for-contemporary-christianity**
101 Harold Percy, *Your Church Can Thrive* (James Bennett, 2003), p. 47.
102 Rick Warren, *Purpose Driven Church* (Zondervan, 1995), p. 111.
103 'What the Leaders Said' (LICC, 2004).
104 See **talkingjesus.org**.
105 Jay Pathak and Dave Runyon, *The Art of Neighbouring* (Baker Books, 2012).
106 Barna, *Evangelism that Works*, ch. 8.
107 Stephen Cottrell, *From the Abundance of the Heart* (DLT, 2006), p. 27.
108 Dallas Willard, *The Divine Conspiracy* (Fount, 1998), p. 334.
109 Willard, *The Divine Conspiracy*, p. 328.
110 Kenneth Scott Latourette, *A History of the Expansion of Christianity*, Vol. 1 (Zondervan, 1976), p. 112.
111 David B. Barrett (ed.), *World Christian Encyclopaedia* (OUP, 2001), p. 3.
112 Graham Tomlin, *The Provocative Church* (SPCK, 2008), ch. 10.
113 *Apprentice 2009*, Spring Harvest/LICC.
114 *Time for Discipleship*, 2014, Evangelical Alliance.
115 See **cultureofinvitation.com**

116 Mark Greene, 'Imagine', LICC, p. 9.

117 Chris Wright, *The Mission of God* (IVP, 2006), p. 35.

118 Willard, *Divine Conspiracy*, p. 309.

119 Willard, *Divine Conspiracy*, p. 311.

120 George Barna, *Maximum Faith* (WHCP, 2011).

121 Michael Wilkins, *Following the Master: A biblical theology of discipleship* (Zondervan,1992), ch. 14.

122 Mark Greene in the foreword to Graham Cray, *Who's Shaping You?* (Cell UK, 2010).

123 Willard, *The Divine Conspiracy*, p. 207.

124 Cray, *Who's Shaping You?*, p. 60.

125 James K.A. Smith, *Desiring the Kingdom* (Baker, 2009), pp. 93–101.

126 Dallas Willard, *Knowing Christ Today* (Harper, 2009), ch. 2.

127 Taylor, *Go-Between God*, p. 3.

128 Taylor, *Go-Between God*, p. 139.

129 Leighton Ford, *The Attentive Life* (IVP, 2008), p. 13.

130 Brother Yun, *The Heavenly Man* (Monarch, 2002), p. 47.

BRF

Transforming
lives and communities

Christian growth and understanding of the Bible

Resourcing individuals, groups and leaders in churches for their own spiritual journey and for their ministry

Church outreach in the local community

Offering two programmes that churches are embracing to great effect as they seek to engage with their local communities and transform lives

Teaching Christianity in primary schools

Working with children and teachers to explore Christianity creatively and confidently

Children's and family ministry

Working with churches and families to explore Christianity creatively and bring the Bible alive

parenting for faith

Visit **brf.org.uk** for more information on BRF's work

brf.org.uk

The Bible Reading Fellowship (BRF) is a Registered Charity (No. 233280)